What people are saying about
A Spirit-Empowered Life . . .

"The Christian life was never meant to be a do-it-yourself project, and thank God it doesn't have to be! The Holy Spirit is here to empower and enable us as we serve God's purpose in our generation. In *A Spirit-Empowered Life,* Dr. Clarensau challenges each of us to welcome the Spirit's work and experience all God has for us in the twenty-first century. This exciting new book will inspire your journey and change your life."

—Dr. Billy Wilson, president of Oral Roberts University

"It seems everyone is looking for something 'extra.' Google 'personal power' and you'll get more than 242,000,000 hits! But that search for personal power is futile—never yielding enough power to manage life and its challenges. *A Spirit-Empowered Life* will help you discover a new way to live. No more searching for your power in books, programs, or from the latest expert. Invest just ten minutes a day for forty days and learn what it means to truly experience power. Thank God, He has a plan for you to live differently, with His power!"

—Rod Loy, senior pastor, First Assembly of God,
North Little Rock, Arkansas;
author of *Three Questions, Immediate Obedience,*
and *After the Honeymoon*

"Incorporating the ministry of the Holy Spirit into contemporary church life has been a challenge for many leaders—often ending up with an unfortunate, passive neglect of His urgently needed help. This book is the roadmap we've been waiting for! *A Spirit-Empowered Life* provides an easily accessible, hunger-driven, biblical process that believers can simply follow to a more fulfilling Christian life."

—Tim Enloe, author, Bible teacher,
Holy Spirit Conferences/Enloe Ministries

"How would you feel if you were one of Christ's disciples and He said: 'I'm leaving; you're staying. Everything you try will be opposed by an adversary; and by the way, you must go out and train everyone you meet to practice all I have commanded you.' Would you feel unprepared? Overwhelmed? Fearful?

If you think this is an impossible mandate, remember that He also said: 'Don't be afraid; I will help you to accomplish what I require.' Natural ability can never produce supernatural results. In his book *A Spirit-Empowered Life* Mike Clarensau will lead you on an exciting journey to a life that is significant, fulfilled, and spiritually effective."

—Alton Garrison, assistant general superintendent
of the General Council of the Assemblies of God

"This book gives Christ-followers an opportunity to find something more than religious tradition. Mike effectively reaches into New Testament days and brings Spirit-empowered living right to the threshold of where we live. Not only is there "more," there is more for you. When addressed, the questions raised in this text will lead the readers into transforming experiences."

—Dr. Paul Brooks, vice president for academics, Southwestern Assemblies
of God University, and professor of Bible and ministry

"Mike Clarensau addresses the issue of empowerment not from a theoretical perspective but from a practicing-Pentecostal perspective. His life embodies what he believes and has practiced. While this alone makes the book worth reading, he also points out how empowerment goes well beyond the verbal and visual gifts of the Spirit. Because there is more, he demonstrates the DNA of the Spirit by addressing relationships, experience, connection, and growth in our walk as believers through the Holy Spirit's empowerment."

—Greg Mundis, executive director, Assemblies of God World Missions

"Mike Clarensau is a gifted writer and storyteller. What adds to the power of his narrative is that what he writes flows out of his passionate and consistent walk with Jesus Christ through the Holy Spirit. This is a book desperately needed in the Spirit-filled family of congregations and will be a valuable source for decades to come!"

—Dr. Doug Beacham, presiding bishop, International Pentecostal Holiness
Church, Oklahoma City, Oklahoma

"One of the most important skills any believer can learn is how to have a relationship with the Holy Spirit. Mike Clarensau has provided a true gift to us in *A Spirit-Empowered Life*, because he uses both real life and biblical examples of how the Holy Spirit can work within us. Each brief chapter is filled with practical and applicable lessons on how to step into this dimension of power in our lives."

—Jeff Leake, lead pastor of Allison Park Church, Pittsburgh, Pennsylvania; author of *God in Motion, The Question That Changed My life, Learning to Follow Jesus,* and *Praying with Confidence*

"We have so much available to us in the baptism and on-going work of the Holy Spirit! Mike has outlined, as only he could, the incredible beauty of a Spirit-empowered life. When we *experience* the Holy Spirit, *yield* to Him, and allow Him to *lead* every part of our lives, we will be transformed. And not only will we be changed, we will positively impact those around us. I join my heart with my husband, and pray for each woman who reads this book—may each of us allow the Holy Spirit to fill us, encourage us, teach us, anoint us, and use us in powerful ways."

—Kerry Clarensau, national women's ministries director, General Council of the Assemblies of God

"When faithful and obedient Christians open themselves to the prospect, they can be filled, or baptized, in the Holy Spirit. This experience is an encounter with the very present God, filling the believer with a keen sense of the daily presence of God—life as He intended. Mike Clarensau, in this theologically sound and immensely practical book, helps readers understand the reality and subsequent outworking of being a Spirit-empowered Christian. Read it and put it in the hands of people who want to understand what it means to be truly Pentecostal."

—Mark L. Williams, general overseer/presiding bishop, Church of God, Cleveland, Tennessee

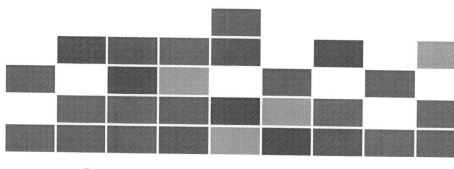

A
SPIRIT-
EMPOWERED
LIFE

Discover the World-Changing Journey
God Has Designed for You

Mike Clarensau

Dedication

I hope this book is somehow worthy to dedicate its pages to Spirit-empowered men and women who have faithfully lived in a way that makes me want what they have. People like my pastors, Gail and Maxine Howard, who shaped and shepherded a church family where I could discover and encounter the living nature of God's promises, are especially in my heart—as are the powerful people who filled the pews around me. The roster of remarkable lives in that place and around the world who have challenged my own is too lengthy to even begin. But their stories, both well known and hidden from view, are the greatest reality heaven has offered.

And yet, I also want to dedicate this book to my granddaughters, Molly Jayne and Lennon Mae, and their future siblings and cousins, 'cause Papa Mike wants them and their friends to find a Spirit-empowered life in their generation, too. As culture seems determined to continue its moral deterioration, I pray that Spirit-empowered people will grow increasingly greater in whatever succeeding generations God's calendar affords us. Hope is tightly attached to the rise of such people, and nothing could be more wonderful than seeing my family's future in the midst of that.

But for today, this book is dedicated to those who live in between—who choose futures and shape worlds now. I want my sons, Tyler and Blake, the girls they spend life with (Katie and Danielle), along with their friends, to know the power I hope I've done more than just write about. Their windshields reveal the destiny laid out for all of us, and we need more Spirit-empowered people in their lifetimes than we have seen in ours. My wife, Kerry, and I dream that for the immediate horizon. We know only the kingdom of God will ultimately endure, and it's the Spirit-empowered who will keep filling that kingdom in each and every generation.

Contents

The Horizon

Foreword

My friend Mike Clarensau has a rich and authentic grasp of the Spirit-filled life. He articulates his perspectives in a way that is both wonderfully inspiring and profoundly practical.

Too often, people misunderstand what it means to be filled with the Spirit. They assume they'll experience some kind of magical power surge. Yes, they'll experience power, but the Holy Spirit's power isn't magic. He tenderly draws us closer to Jesus, imparts the heart of Jesus, and gives us the desire to serve like Jesus. At every moment, Jesus was intimately connected to the Father, doing what the Father told Him to do, and saying what the Father told Him to say. For Jesus, life was a divine encounter—a loving, powerful relationship. Jesus lived the Spirit-filled life. If we want to know what it means to be Spirit-filled, we need to look at Jesus.

As the Spirit led Jesus, He had divine encounters with the rich and powerful as well as the poor and needy. No one was beyond the reach of His love, truth, and power. As we experience the presence, purpose, and power of the Spirit of God, He will lead us on the greatest adventure of our lives. He will speak to us, and He will speak through us. We'll love the people who intimidate others by their power—but we won't be afraid because we know Someone with infinite power. And we'll love the people others overlook—because we are amazed that Jesus didn't overlook us.

Our divine connection with God and His divine mandate are clearly spelled out in the Gospels.

Before Christ ascended, He told His followers:

> Go into all the world and preach the gospel to all cre-
> ation. Whoever believes and is baptized will be saved,
> but whoever does not believe will be condemned. And
> these signs will accompany those who believe: In my
> name they will drive out demons; they will speak in new
> tongues; they will pick up snakes with their hands; and

when they drink deadly poison, it will not hurt them at
all; they will place their hands on sick people, and they
will get well. (Mark 16:15–18)

We don't have to wonder what the Spirit-filled life looks like. Jesus
said it includes:

Divine purpose: We represent the glorious King and Savior to a lost
and dying world. Others may sell them technology, a new car, or a million
other things, but we offer the free gift of grace, the assurance of forgiveness,
a new purpose for living, and the certain hope of eternal life. God could have
written His message to the world in the sky, or He could have sent angels,
but He chose us to be His voice, His hands, and His feet to take the Good
News to every corner of the globe.

Divine power: We don't go in our own strength. The battle is far
too great for us! But the mighty Spirit of God lives in us to give us the
power to battle Satan and his dark angels. With the power of the Spirit, we
resist temptation in ourselves and warn others of its dangers; we identify
deception and counter it with God's truth; and we stand our ground when
the devil accuses us because we claim the righteousness of Jesus Christ
that He imparted to us when we believed.

Divine communication: Spirit-filled believers have supernatural intimacy with God. In fact, we have our own language, given to us by God so we
can know Him more fully. As we pray in the Spirit, God gives us assurance,
direction, and hope so that all we do is infused with His purpose and power.

Divine protection: Those who opposed Jesus often threatened Him.
The history of the church tells us that people often reject a bold, loving
proclamation of the gospel, and God's messengers are sometimes beaten and
killed. Ironically, the Prince of Peace is a lightning rod for fierce opposition.
It's not a popular message in our self-saturated culture, but suffering is part
of the walk of faith for those who are sold out to Jesus. In our struggle, we
have God's assurance that we won't endure more than we can handle. This
gives us a new concept of "God's favor." When we suffer because we love
the way Jesus loved, speak the truth the way Jesus spoke, and serve the
way Jesus served, we're right in the middle of God's perfect will, which is
the essence of God's divine favor.

Divine healing: Psychologists and nurses tell us that human touch
has healing properties. Those who are filled with the Spirit know that the
laying on of hands infuses touch with supernatural love and strength to heal

physical sickness and emotional wounds. God may heal some instantly or He may take more time to heal others, but healing is an integral part of the kingdom of God on earth.

All of this is God's gracious gift *to us*, and it is God's gift *through us* as we represent Him to our family, friends, coworkers, strangers, and everyone else we touch in our neighborhoods and around the world. God gives each of us the power to be this kind of person, this kind of Christ-follower, in every sphere of our relationships.

One of the misconceptions about the Spirit-filled life is that we somehow float above life's difficulties and become immune to heartache and struggle. Actually, walking with the Spirit gives us more humility so we can admit when we fail, when we resist the Spirit's promptings, and when we're confused about His leading. God doesn't expect perfection from those who love Him and give their lives to Him! I'm so encouraged to see how Jesus related to those who ran away on the night He was betrayed, the one who denied Him three times, and those who somehow failed to get the message of His repeated explanations that He would be killed but rise again. After the resurrection, the disciples hid in fear for their lives, but Jesus sought them out, came to them, and assured them again and again that He had something special for them. His love never fails . . . even though we often do. As we're filled with the Spirit, we're more honest, more compassionate, more humble, and more joyful—more like Jesus.

Mike Clarensau lives the principles and practices described in this book. His faith is vibrant and alive, and his insights challenge and motivate. As you read and study this book, ask God to meet you and inflame your heart with love for Christ. And listen. Listen for the whisper and the shout of the Spirit, and follow wherever He leads. God will use you in incredible ways. It'll be the greatest adventure you could ever experience.

—Scott Wilson, senior pastor of The Oaks Fellowship,
Red Oak, Texas

Introduction

I've spent my entire life as a part of a Pentecostal church. Hearing people talk about a life driven by the power of the Holy Spirit, illustrated through the compelling characters described in the Bible or stories lived as recently as today, dominates my earliest memories and has significantly shaped my understanding of God and His plan for those who serve Him. As a child, I sat mesmerized by the tales of missionaries, bursting with amazement at their victories and wiping tears as their compassion cultivated something similar in me. I've cheered healings and celebrated expressions of faith, sometimes amidst headlines and sometimes unknown beyond our circle. A life in the Spirit surrounded me, repeatedly urging me to cross its threshold with potentials I could only begin to dream of.

The promise of such a life seems to be a grandiose expectation thrust upon this book by its title. But I've seen such a life and watched as others have responded to its call, engaging a journey of God's power and presence that exceeded any day they had previously lived. Can it really be? It can and is and will continue to be.

I was nine years old the first time Acts 2:4 became my living reality. Perhaps you wonder if that moment with my friends at a church camp subsequently launched me to greater spiritual heights—to encounter a bit of what I write about. I hope that it has, but spotting a Spirit-filled life is typically something others do. I can more easily see it in you than in me. You see, the Spirit-empowered seldom find reason to speak of themselves. Instead, they live in a continual hunger, wanting to draw closer, longing to reach beyond what their hands have previously touched. They tend to speak more of the God who has called and equipped them than they try to squeeze inside the edges of a spotlight He alone deserves.

But, like thousands across my nation and even millions around the world, I do know the path to that upper room and the life that it promises. I can find myself in the confused but committed disciples as they tried to process an overwhelming mission. And I can almost see Jesus' passion and the way His final instructions paved the road that gave their futures its direction.

What I know, I have used to shape this book. As the opening section reveals, the pursuit begins with *hunger*. God has opened an extraordinary door to us, adorned with remarkable promises, but until we find reason to choose, until our desire and recognition of our need explosively combine, we will stay on the sidelines among those who struggle to find the abundant life they thought a connection to God would bring. As you will see, everything starts with hunger.

By the way, I've included some questions to *think about* at the end of each chapter. Use these to explore your own hunger or to go a bit deeper into the thoughts I only have pages to introduce. I hope you'll do more than just read this book. Instead, challenge yourself to fully engage the journey these pages will unfold by taking time to reflect and explore every step along the way.

Encounter is our second section—the moment when promise melts into fulfillment and the God who once shook every building He entered now consumes us with similar results. The Spirit-empowered discover that everything ultimately flows from the side-by-side spigots of relationship and experience. The God we know and will continually know more arrives ahead of our challenges to pour into our lives what He knows we must pour out. This life isn't captured by the dream of pleasing God with how we live, but learning how He can live within and through our moments in ways that show more of Him than us. When that begins to happen, adjectives run short. The God who proved Himself powerful among those early disciples demonstrates that His work is unfinished and His strategy has encompassed folks as unlikely in our generation as they were in theirs.

The largest section of this book describes the *demonstration* of such a life. How do Spirit-empowered people live? What makes them different as they connect, grow, and serve? What drives them forward, and how do they express themselves to the God who has sent them forth? These are not traits to aspire to but the fruit that readily falls from a vine with such power within. The demonstration is what we see when God's Spirit fills a person.

Our final pages describe the *horizon* for those who live that power. Where do we focus? What do we prioritize? If the demonstration is the fruit of our tree, then the next steps describe how that tree is tended, cared for, and perpetuated. (By the way, we have created additional tools to help you live a Spirit-empowered life. You can find these at the back of the book.)

Make no mistake—our God's unbounded creativity is often best seen in the unique journeys He has imagined for each of us. But the road to find that life can be familiarly marked. Otherwise, we couldn't help one another pursue God's absolute best in our lives. I hope I can help you as you explore these pages, because I genuinely want you to find a Spirit-empowered life.

But I guarantee that God wants that even more!

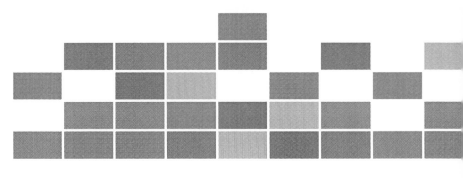

THE HUNGER

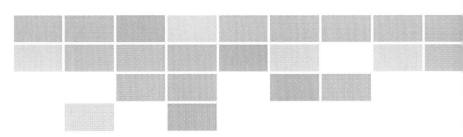

CHAPTER

1

Stories

*T*his is crazy! The thought had to be bursting through his mind. Just days ago, a man had appeared in the north cave with a message too hard for the young man to believe. How could he possibly put an end to the terrorism his people had experienced for nearly a decade? He wanted to believe, but there were dozens of stronger men—men people would follow, men people would believe in.

People were already mad at him. Last night he had smashed the community altar, likely bringing the wrath of the many strange gods worshipped there. His own dad had kept an angry mob from dragging him into the streets, but he knew it was only a matter of time until they found him. And it seemed like he was about to help them do just that.

Now the young man's sweaty fingers squeezed the trumpet in his hand. He knew the next few moments might well be his last, but somehow he couldn't bring himself to run. Then suddenly, somehow, the trembling young man knew he wasn't alone. Something . . . no, *someone* was there. Quickly, his eyes darted up and down all sides of the hill where he stood. There was no one there . . . but he knew there was . . . Someone.

At that moment, he thrust the horn to his mouth, not in panic but in newfound determination. With a force greater than any lung capacity he'd ever felt, he blew the long, clear call to battle. The sound pierced the air above the valley, lingering and echoing long after the trumpet fell to his side. In the distance, he could see warriors emerging from their homes. They grasped swords and spears as they ran toward the sound of the trumpet. For a moment, the young man wanted to run, but a steeled determination rooted his feet to that hill until the ground below began to fill with the strongest men even a greater general could muster.

In that moment, this reluctant soldier was launched into the most re-markable battle in human history. Though ultimately outnumbered nearly five hundred to one, his forces destroyed the entire enemy army with battle methods never used before or since. A mere 300 men had routed 135,000 enemy soldiers led by the most unlikely of warriors. But there *was* something about him . . . something beating inside that frightened plow-boy that made him a giant in military history.

How? The historian who penned the story could only say, "The Spirit of the LORD came on Gideon" (Judg. 6:34).

It happened again!

Samson could feel his muscles tighten, as if something inside him was about to explode. He twisted left and right, and the ropes his own countrymen had tied around him to deliver him to the enemy fell weakly to the ground. His captors, a few Philistine leaders and the troops that served them, saw the ropes fall and reached for their swords with terror in their eyes. But they weren't quick enough.

Samson already held the facial bone of a donkey in his hand and swung the bleached bone across the skull of the nearest soldier. The sickening thud stirred dozens of others, but he was on them before they could wield their weapons. In minutes, more than a hundred Philistine warriors lay dead at the feet of the slightly built but remarkably powerful Israelite.

Samson kept swinging, as though his arms might never tire. Indeed, the strength he felt surging through his shoulders showed no sign of abating. No matter how many enemy warriors lunged toward him, he repelled each one with seeming ease, and the power of his slashing strokes was too much for both their armor and the bones that lay beneath. As the Philistine soldiers crumpled to the ground, their eyes betrayed their final thoughts as they stared in amazement at the man who was unlike any they had ever seen. But in a few seconds, the amazed looks turned cold with death.

Soon the battle was over, a thousand Philistine bodies offering the evidence of a single man's strength (Judg. 15:14–15). A few remaining soldiers ran from the scene and Samson tossed the donkey bone aside with a laugh, choosing not to chase after them. After all, the stories those frightened solders would tell in their cities might be just what was needed to keep the Philistines from raiding Israelite villages for a while. He wiped the blood from his arms and laughed at how a donkey's jawbone had made donkeys of a once-powerful army.

Samson was a man with a secret—one that occasionally burst forth in unbelievable power. First, he had shredded a lion with his bare hands (14:6), massacred the men who had stolen and later killed his wife (vv. 19–20), and lifted the gates of a great city from their hinges (16:3). Philistine fields remained charred from the day he set foxes running with fire burning from their tails (15:4–5).

These were the exploits of giants, of men whose muscles threatened to burst from beneath their tunics. But Samson was no giant. To meet him was to be unimpressed by his size, likely assuming the stories were myths, the result of carefully crafted Israeli propaganda. But too many had seen him in action to slow the spread of his legend.

He seemed no different than the other men of his village, save the unruly long hair and unshaven face. What could cause such an average man to explode with greater strength than two teams of horses?

Those who told his story stated simply, "The Spirit of the LORD came powerfully upon him" (Judg. 15:14).

They had left him in the fields

It's not easy being the youngest of eight brothers, always being pushed aside or wrestled to the ground by their more-developed muscles. For David, life as the little brother had largely been what one would imagine—a test of endurance and lots of bruises.

That's why he eagerly embraced his father's assignment to care for the family flocks. Being able to avoid his brothers and their apparent need to prove their dominant place was a welcomed break. Besides, the cool grass and refreshing ponds had often been the perfect backdrop to the music he loved to play. The sheep seemed to like it, too.

But today wasn't like other days. Word had spread among the other shepherds that the prophet Samuel had come to Jesse's house, apparently to anoint a new king for Israel. David could only imagine the excitement dancing in his father's eyes and the scrambling of the entire household as they prepared for such a magnificent event. *So Eliab will be king*, David thought. He imagined his other brothers watching with envy, wondering if by some miracle the assignment might be taken from their eldest brother and thrust onto their shoulders. He could almost picture them wanting to wrestle Eliab to the ground one more time before Samuel's anointing oil swelled both his rank and his head with plans for a kingdom. Well, David would know soon enough. Surely a messenger would appear on the horizon in a few moments, summoning young David for the family event.

But the morning came and went with no word from home. Had the prophet not arrived? Why hadn't they come for him? Surely, his brother was being celebrated at this very moment, but neither word nor invitation had come.

Finally as the afternoon sun beat hard against David's puzzled brow, a servant came running toward the flock, carelessly scattering the sheep in his rush. The shepherds scolded him angrily, but his gaze was so fixed on David that he seemed unaware of their curses.

"Is my brother anointed to be king?" David asked, assuming he had been forgotten amid the day's excitement.

"The prophet has sent for you," the servant spoke in a barely audible tone as he pulled David back toward the hill. Confused and full of questions, David followed quickly after the servant. The larger man's silent strides told David he would have to get his answers from someone at home.

That day everything changed for young David. The forgotten son of Jesse would never be forgotten again as Samuel lifted the pitcher of oil above his head and poured it liberally into David's curly hair. As that thick mixture rolled down David's cheeks and began to drip into his sandals, something happened. Those who tell the story simply said, "The Spirit of the LORD came powerfully upon David" (1 Sam. 16:13).

What does that mean? For David it meant a lion and a bear would be no match for his determined strength. He wrestled each of these would-be sheep stealers to the ground, breaking their necks with technique that would amaze his older brothers. It meant even a giant Philistine warrior who held Israel's entire army in paralyzed fear would be no match for him and the missile-like stone he thrust from a small sling. He needed no armor, no battle plan, no backup forces. The boy they had ignored and left in the fields now conquered every challenge all by himself.

Or perhaps not. Like Gideon, Samson, and a few others before him, David won the most unlikely victories with the most remarkable strength. Like those great warriors of old, David held no impressive credentials and had little reason to believe he could have such capacity. There is only one explanation—an explanation held in common with the greatest of the Bible's champions.

The Spirit of the Lord came powerfully upon him.

THINK ABOUT IT

1. Which of the stories of Spirit-empowered individuals impresses you most and why?
2. Why do you suppose God would choose such ordinary people to do extraordinary things?
3. If your strength had no limit, what would you want to do for God?

CHAPTER 2

There's Gotta Be More . . .

I want more! I'm not greedy, and I don't think I tip the self-centered scale any further than other folks, but I want more—a lot more.

Okay, perhaps I should back up a bit, because the desire for more can be both good and bad. More time to be helpful and more stuff to share with others seem like appropriate desires, but more bacon at breakfast or a lot more of the green stuff to spend on myself probably won't be good for my overall health. The idea of more needs a bit of definition before you would be willing to offer a hearty "me too."

If I launched into all the "mores" I wish I could obtain, I'm sure the list would span more than a few pages—yours would, too. Any time good things come our way, we naturally hope for more, don't we? More pay, more good neighbors, more opportunities, more time with family, and certainly more vacation time all sound like winners to me. But the "more" that propels me to write these words is a deep desire for something else . . . more . . . *life!*

Now before you think I'm dreaming of an extended stay on this most attractive of all planets, let me clarify a bit. Quantity of life, while not a bad thing to want more of, isn't what I'm after. Instead, my idea of "more life" has something to do with quality. I want to unearth the path to life on the highest plane, to live the life I was made for, to find a fulfillment and purpose that lifts me above normal or average and into something that matters, well . . . even more.

Jesus said we could have that kind of life. He claimed to have come that we "may have life, and have it to the full" (John 10:10). Hundreds of the Bible's pages tell stories of that kind of life—a life that somehow seems to elude us in spite of our tweetable wisdoms, ever-evolving cultures, and increasingly superior technologies.

Eugene Peterson, in his excellent little book, *Run with Horses,* describes the realities of modern life with tragic accuracy:

> The puzzle is why so many people live so badly. Not so wickedly, but so inanely. Not so cruelly, but so stupidly. There is little to admire and less to imitate in the people who are prominent in our culture. We have celebrities but not saints. Famous entertainers amuse a nation of bored insomniacs. Infamous criminals act out the aggressions of timid conformists. Petulant and spoiled athletes play games vicariously for lazy and apathetic spectators. People, aimless and bored, amuse themselves with trivia and trash. Neither the adventure of goodness nor the pursuit of righteousness gets headlines.[1]

What an indictment of our modern times! And Peterson wrote those words before reality TV and other less than compelling fare took over the airwaves. In fact, thirty years have elapsed since he penned those words, and we'd be hard-pressed to prove we've made any progress in a better direction.

Shouldn't there be more?

After stunning me with his compelling first paragraph, Peterson went on to introduce me to an Old Testament verse that's been my favorite ever since. Though hidden amidst the complicated stories of even more complicated prophetic books, this little verse triggers a much-needed hope and thirst for more than what I see around me.

> If you have raced with men on foot and they have worn you out, how can you compete with horses? If you stumble in safe country, how will you manage in the thickets by the Jordan? (Jer. 12:5)

I was enjoying a couple of breakfast burritos at my neighborhood McDonald's when the idea of running with horses leapt from the page, causing me to drop the hash browns I was preparing to bite. *Run with horses? Is that really what God wanted Jeremiah to do?*

Like you, I was pretty sure the idea was figurative. After all, horses are big, and fast, and those long strides would leave even the fastest human in the dust. I'm a city kid who got bucked off a Shetland pony at age five so I'm hardly a horse whisperer, but I've seen enough Kentucky Derby races on TV to know they'd be finishing the race before I made it to the first turn.

The reason my breakfast side dish suddenly plummeted back to the tray isn't that I've always dreamed of sprinting across open fields, amazing the drivers in passing cars. But in that instant, I knew God was offering Jeremiah something I wanted as well. The infinite Creator was telling His diminutive friend, *There's more!* Somehow there was life above and beyond the grind that was wearing out that frustrated prophet. Somehow he could find a race on a different level than the rats around him were running. And it seems from God's invitation that Jeremiah was meant for that greater race.

I swallowed the rest of my breakfast that morning and decided that I would find that life. If there was any chance that God's invitation to Jeremiah remained open to the rest of us, then I wanted to run with horses . . . and I still do.

Do you?

The remaining pages of this book offer a road map for finding and ultimately living that kind of life. But before there's any chance you can find the right highway, you have to resolve what may be the most critical issue of the journey: *You have to want it.*

You see, most of us came to God out of an awareness of our need. Whether in crisis circumstances or amidst the calm reality of our daily existence, we recognized that we needed more than just us. The limits of our resources awakened us to our needs and someone pointed us to the hope they had found in connecting with God. Guilt, sickness, stress, brokenness, anxiety, and even death can be great teachers. They underscore the God-sized hole inside each of us—the one He put there for His future lodging—that we may have tried filling in numerous unsatisfactory ways. Though our stories differ and our routes to the needed revelation may be filled with varying levels of failure and subsequent devastation, still it was need that brought us to our knees.

I hadn't been to school yet when I figured out I needed God. But I'd been to Sunday school . . . a lot. Between Sunday mornings, Sunday evenings, and Wednesday's midweek services, I'd logged well over 600 hours in church by my third birthday. That's a lot of time being told by kind-hearted people that Jesus loved me and that I needed Him in my life. When I was old enough to agree with them, probably somewhere around the 800-hour mark, I jumped into this journey with both feet. I needed God and He wanted me, so the first steps of connection were launched.

Others take a different route to discover their need for God. I have friends who didn't log hundreds of church hours as a kid. Instead, theirs was a pretty bumpy ride through disappointments, insecurities, rebellions, and a few tragic decisions. For them, realizing need wasn't the hard part. It just took awhile before someone told them about God. When that finally happened, they were quick to respond—some only required one hour in church to find what they were looking for.

No matter what the road you traveled toward God looked like, it was your need that fueled the journey. But there's a greater step beyond that critical precipice. If you're going to find a life of more—the abundant one Jesus spoke of and the greater race God offered His prophet—you have to *really want it.*

Hunger is a critical element in the journey with God. Many people can recognize their need for God, and thankfully He has proven His willingness to fill our voids; however, it seems that the roster of those who want to know Him is a bit shorter. The apostle Paul was on that list. Though he had lived many amazing moments and achieved more for God than most of us dream of, he was still saying, "I want to know Christ—yes, to know the power of his resurrection" (Phil. 3:10). You'd think the old guy had already hit the highest places of his journey, but he wanted more!

Hunger talks.

No, I don't mean the hunger that causes your stomach to make embarrassing noises a few minutes before lunch hour. But hunger, real hunger for a deeper relationship with God, shouts more than a few powerful statements through your attitudes and actions.

Hunger says . . . *the life that seems normal doesn't appeal to me.* With hunger, there's a longing for something beyond what is easy to reach. Anyone can settle for what is common. Most people seem to live average, somewhat self-centered lives. They look for contentment and pleasure in places crowded by fellow-seekers and somehow miss the lack of satisfaction found there. Hunger stays awake to the dissatisfaction of this "normal" existence and pushes toward something deeper.

How many people need to crash and burn on the money and power trip before they wake up to the inadequacy of such a life? For generations, people have been finding that road to be empty and dissatisfying, often depriving its travelers of the most important relationships in their lives. Must people keep playing a game where the winners end up losing? Hunger says, "No thanks," and breaks from the mold in search of a better path.

Hunger says . . . *knowing God has become the passion of my life.* The discovery of God and the opportunity to connect with Him has to be the most compelling of human experiences. Can you imagine truly knowing

God—I mean connecting to Him in a real relationship? Hunger imagines the possibilities and quickly abandons other paths to chase such potential.

If life is more than the result of cosmic accidents and random mutations, and if there's a purpose and a Purposer—a Designer who's massive enough to make all this and make me, too—then discovering Him and embracing a journey through the questions that follow makes far more sense than living to pay off a mortgage. Hunger recognizes the endless capacity for wonder in the idea of a God who wants to be known. How could that journey ever become boring?

Hunger says . . . *I believe God has something greater for my life.* Could there be a greater purpose than the one an eternal God has designed? Can any other agenda compare with the importance of His? We all long for the significance of knowing our lives matter, and most of us spend our best energy looking for such meaning. Hunger knows that the Maker of life is likely the One with the best plan for living it.

In Isaiah 6:1–8, the great prophet finds himself in the overwhelming scene around God's throne. Quickly recognizing that he's exposed by the white-hot holiness of the One he longs to know, he cannot move until his weakness is lifted, an act of mercy somehow extended to him. But Isaiah's focus quickly shifts from himself as he hears the same voice that soothed his failures express an even higher agenda— "Whom shall I send? And who will go for us?" Isaiah thrusts his hand upward, longing to embrace the mission of the One who had cleansed him. What journey could matter more? Hunger grasps the wonder of one so limited being entrusted with the purposes of the Eternal.

Hunger says . . . *I want more.*

THINK ABOUT IT

1. In what way did need bring you to Christ?
2. What are you truly hungry for? Describe your hunger in a few sentences.

CHAPTER 3

Tired of Learning and Doing

Those who are living remarkable lives with God—crashing through the limits of common existence, encountering the outer edges of human experience, and tiptoeing through the occasional supernatural moment—should have the most amazing stories. How is it that too many of us have become bored with our faith and find the settings where we worship God with others to be tame and monotonous? A good friend of mine often says, "It's a sin to make the Bible boring." I'm afraid we may have done even worse. We've made the journey with God seem like a real yawner.

How can a connection with God become boring? It's easy to imagine how Christianity could be challenging, compelling, and at times, overwhelming, but how can a life fueled by the presence of God have become so unattractive to the millions who know it's available?

Since I can't imagine that God has lost interest, it's perhaps best to assume that we're responsible for the current state of Christianity in the Western world. Empty cathedrals and powerless church services seem an unlikely product of a God who desires to make Himself known. There's got to be another culprit—and I think it must be us.

Today, it seems our Christianity is defined largely by what we know and what we do. We engage classroom settings where we learn the facts about God and comb through the cultural import of biblical accounts until we understand what Moses was thinking when he stood before Pharaoh, why Samuel was ticked with Saul for his disobedience, and why it's a good thing that Paul ended up in Macedonia rather than fighting his way through Bithynia. We puzzle at Abraham's marriage to his half-sister and wonder why he lied about it, apparently willing to trade her for peace in a foreign land. We adopt our own theories about the giants in Genesis 6, though the flood made them irrelevant to daily life just one chapter later.

Now, I'm all for biblical knowledge and lost count long ago of the hours I've spent studying God's Book and trying to teach it to others. Learning is a good thing, especially when the content is of eternal value. But learning separated from living reality is just brain exercise that does your feet little good.

That kind of learning seems void of the living, doesn't it? Celebrating David's rock finding its mark in Goliath's forehead is a lot of fun, but why don't my rocks find such supernatural trajectory? I can imagine the excitement of abundant loaves and fishes at Jesus' first-century picnic, but I've been to church dinners where we ran out of food and had to send a few disciples to a nearby store. And yes, I know it was a boon to the Jerusalem saints when Peter raised Tabitha from the dead. They needed her skills to care for so many in need, but I've said goodbye to my share of Tabithas. I needed them also, but I have never ended a funeral with an empty casket.

You see, I don't want to just read the stories and master the details of their original contexts. I have no reluctance for learning and would never label any Bible study as wasted effort. It's just that I want more than the chance to memorize these miraculous historical events. I want to live them, and I think God wants that, too.

The other side of Christianity's modern coin is the doing. When James told us not to simply listen to the word but to do what it says (1:22), we took him seriously. So today's local church offers a calendar with enough activities to exhaust those Genesis 6 giants. We didn't get labels like "do-gooders" without doing stuff, and the good stuff we do is what gives the local church its best reputation.

But all this doing is exhausting and not always fulfilling. While each of us gains a measure of satisfaction when we help someone in need, it's often difficult to distinguish the evidence of

> Unless we've somehow eclipsed the relevance of the Bible, I think it's safe to conclude that God intended to do stuff in our generation, too.

God in many of our efforts. We do what we can (praying God will bless it), but meeting needs tends to breed more needs, and our capacity seldom proves to be anything possessing a truly God-sized potential.

Now we'll say a lot more about this learning and doing model of Christianity in later chapters, but can we agree that there seems to be a sizeable gap between our efforts and those of the original church members, a power gap that many of us are desperate to bridge?

I'm not content to write off such potential with the idea that we don't need God's supernatural activity like they did centuries ago. Unless we've somehow eclipsed the relevance of the Bible, I think it's safe to conclude that God intended to do stuff in our generation, too. Stories of amazing realities on other continents show His many fingerprints. It seems defeating to conjure theological ideas that eliminate the possibility that we could experience something similar.

I want more.

Many years ago, a few folks decided that following Christ could best be accomplished in less than accessible settings. Now, I'm no expert on the passion behind monastic life and I'm certainly not going to criticize its various achievements, but there was nothing withdrawn or distant about Jesus. He spent most of His days neck-deep in people stuff. Lepers with their oozing sores, beggars both unkempt and supremely malodorous, and those "riff-raff" ignored by the religious folks were more common in Jesus' traveling party than the lovely and sweet-smelling. When He left His place in God's throne room and came to live among us, He didn't pick a resort. Bethlehem, Nazareth, Galilee, and even Jerusalem were much better known for their huddled masses than for their vacation brochures.

And when He handed off the mission to the apostles, their worlds didn't look much different. Most didn't have to go far to start using that "ends of the earth" label. But as they went, their lives of power mirrored the one they'd seen Jesus live. Someone wisely observed that they turned the world upside down. You can't do that without touching it.

But touching it is the whole point, isn't it? Jesus launched His disciples with the idea that they would change the world, that His power would be evident in their lives, and that they would go far beyond their own capacities and do amazing things in His name. You see, this is a relationship with God, a life empowered by His remarkable presence. When such a life touches earth, how can the results be anything short of stunning?

He's God, right? So how can the immense Ruler of all things step into our lives without making things amazing? Shouldn't there be evidence of His presence in us, an evidence that shows up in more than just our ideas about Him or a to-do list He's signed off on? How can God be in the house without messing up the house a little bit?

Here's where I think many of us miss the point. We see our connection with God as cleaning up our current act so we can start over, reinitiate the path of our wisest thinking, and see if we can do better this time. Surely there's more to this encounter than that!

In the days of the tabernacle, Moses would emerge from conversation with God sporting a remarkable glow. His brother, Aaron, and those who followed him in the priestly function, would enter the holiest place each year to provide a critical sacrifice. Every detail of that process had to be followed precisely so the priest would survive. They even tied a rope around his ankle so they could drag him out in case he didn't. Now I know Jesus showed us a more approachable way to the Father, but shouldn't there still be something life-changing when we encounter Him, and shouldn't the connection offer similar hope of change for the world around us?

It seems we've isolated the purposes of God into a transaction we can engage with a single-sentence prayer. "Say this" or "repeat after me" has taken center stage in the effort to know God. Complete the sentence, join our next class, and help us hand out bulletins next week has replaced any real sense of spiritual life. If we are encountering God, there has to be more, right?

We can add Jesus' expectations to our argument for more, too. Even as He was performing life-altering miracles, shocking crowds with His power over sickness, showing His authority over the elements of nature, and even disrupting funerals by giving life to the corpse, Jesus told His disciples (and us by proxy) that we would do "greater things" (John 14:12). How's that for a promise?

We assume He didn't mean "greater" in the qualitative sense. It's hard to top raising the dead, changing the weather with a command, or removing lepers from the ranks of the unclean. We might be able to suggest some impressive feats, but I can't see how anything could truly be greater than what He did.

So we take "greater" to mean quantity. Jesus started with twelve guys, so if He gave them His authority and power, they could be in twelve locations rather than just the one they had shared with Him. And, of course, there's a bunch of us who have determined to follow Him, too, so "greater" can potentially mean multiplied millions of things if we can engage the life He offered.

I want more, and I know there has to be more. All the signs seem to be pointing there. Can you see that? Even more importantly, do you want that?

THINK ABOUT IT

1. Has your journey with God been truly compelling? Or have things slowed a bit over the years?
2. Do you think you're living the "abundant life" Jesus came to offer?

CHAPTER 4

Power and Authority

The life Jesus demonstrated and placed before us has to be more than what many of us are living. Just before He returned to heavenly places, Jesus left His disciples with these words:

> Then Jesus came to them and said, "All authority in heaven and on earth has been given to me. Therefore go and make disciples of all nations, baptizing them in the name of the Father and of the Son and of the Holy Spirit, and teaching them to obey everything I have commanded you. And surely I am with you always, to the very end of the age." (Matt. 28:18–20)

We Christians recognize our mission statement in these words. We have frequently challenged one another with the commission to "go and make disciples," launching numerous efforts toward this worldwide challenge. But we typically spend less time considering the previous sentence. Jesus' opening line in this missional command says something powerful about power, and the clear implication is that our ability to fulfill the rest of the paragraph hinges on this first sentence.

"All authority in heaven and on earth" sounds like quite a bit of authority, doesn't it? Now most of us are quick to approve the idea of giving Jesus such authority. After all, He had just finished dying for the sins of the world and a now-empty tomb offered sufficient evidence that He was not an ordinary guy. He is eternally more than that. So His claim that God had given Him all authority seems appropriate. But how did He plan to use that authority?

His first exercise of this ruling power is found in these important words. What was His plan? Well, it seems there are two possibilities. First, He might have been using this authority to command His disciples to fulfill His mission. In other words, "I've proven I'm God, now do what I say or else!" Without question, He would have every right to make such a demand, but that doesn't seem to fit with the tone we've seen previously in His servant-style leadership.

Now I don't want to leave this possible interpretation too quickly. Many people see the Great Commission in such tones. This is the life directive; the insistence seems only to be missing an opening "thou shalt." While all of us should find our sense of calling in words like these, how we read them says a lot about how we view the One who called. I have no problem with the idea that the One who gave me life has a right to dictate how I use it, but elsewhere He's made my choice important. So rather than thinking Jesus is using His authority to boss us all around, I think He must mean something else in that opening line.

That other option says that Jesus will use His authority to equip and empower us as we obey His words. Yes, He has a right to demonstrate power over us, but the real use of that authority is to help us overcome any obstacle that might hinder us in fulfilling the Commission.

For approximately three years, the disciples had seen Jesus use His Father's authority to command storms, sicknesses, and situations in stunning fashion. Now Jesus has been given that authority, seemingly so His disciples can reveal similar power in His name. So, in Acts 3, a lame man walks for the first time when two of the disciples offer him healing in Jesus' name. Later, life returns to the aforementioned Tabitha through that same authority, and other miracles that mirror Jesus' own moments take place as these newly launched apostles encounter their own moments.

Both from the context of Jesus' ministry and the subsequent results we see in the disciples' stories, it seems clear that Jesus was promising to use His authority as the means to fulfill His Great Commission.

For further proof, Jesus wrapped up the commissioning paragraph with a promise to be with the disciples always. Now that's great news, but if He just means He will keep an eye on them and make sure they're doing what He said, then maybe it's not such good news. I suppose Jesus could be saying, "I'll be watching you," like a mom who's less than confident that her kids will behave when she leaves the room.

But if that's His plan, then He must think we are capable of fulfilling His Commission without any intervention on His part. So He tells us what to do and plans to watch, perhaps recording the names of any slackers in a big book. That would make Jesus the foreman on what we will find is an impossible job, but it's ours to do anyway. Doesn't that seem unlikely?

Honestly, I don't want Jesus tailing me unless He's going to do stuff—stuff like helping me when my efforts to obey Him prove insufficient. (I'm approaching half a century of full-time effort in this assignment, and I can tell you that the moments of insufficiency aren't getting any less frequent.) My boots have been on the ground long enough to know supernatural air strikes are needed.

Jesus' promise of His presence with His followers and with those of us who live a bit closer to the end of the age isn't a threat. It's good news! We can't do this without Him! And the statement in Matthew 18:18 demonstrates that He never intended us to act alone. He plans to empower us, to equip us, and to use His well-earned authority on our behalf. After all, it's still His mission and the apostle Paul reminds us that it's our joy to be "called according to his purpose" (Rom. 8:28).

While we don't take Jesus' claim of authority as a demand for our obedience, we shouldn't assume a careless posture either. The kingdom we've been invited to join comes with a missional assignment for every member. Jesus' commission isn't the task of a few, an assignment shared only if we are willing to lay aside our more self-centered pursuits, or the work expected only of the exceptionally devout. Every disciple shares in this calling. It's Jesus' mission, but He made it clear that His disciples share in this same assignment.

One of the most vivid metaphors describing the purpose of Jesus' incarnation is His statement, "I am the light of the world" (John 8:12). Given the obvious darkness that has shadowed a sinful world, the imagery of light isn't hard to understand. Jesus came as light—that's what John the Baptist told us, too (1:8).

> The kingdom we've been invited to join comes with a missional assignment for every member.

But the aforementioned text says that John the Baptist wasn't the light but was sent "as a witness" to that light. His work was to help people prepare for the coming of that light. We'll say more about the assignment given to this interesting character in a later section, but for now we need to see that the Baptist had a role in launching Jesus' mission, but he had not been given Jesus' mission.

For you and me, things are a bit different. Jesus' mission is our mission. He came to be the Light of the world, but Jesus Himself gave His disciples the same mission. He made disciples of the original dozen and several more and then commissioned them (and us) to make disciples of all nations. He came "to seek and to save the lost" (Luke 19:10) and then sent them (us, too) to the ends of the earth in search of the same quarry.

In Matthew 5:14, He calls us the "light of the world," too! And the authority He claims is the means by which we can fulfill His mission. Doesn't that reshape thoughts about your life a little bit? You and I have been called to share in Jesus' eternal mission, and Jesus has been given all authority and will demonstrate His power through us so we can fulfill this immense purpose, in spite of our normal human limitations.

That's why Jesus wanted His disciples to know about the authority He had been given. Jesus was about to launch these simple characters on the most amazing mission ever given to folks like us, and He knew they would be overwhelmed by the task at hand. Few, if any, of them had ever traveled beyond their local borders or had a real conversation with someone from another culture. How could they possibly spread Jesus' message to "the ends of the earth" (Acts 1:8)? For some, their own families didn't understand their choice to abandon life's current course to follow this peasant preacher. How would they speak to kings and prominent people in far off locales?

When you read the subsequent exploits of these simple men, whether in the book of Acts or through some of the ancient texts of church history, it's hard not to be impressed by their courage and the force that propelled them into the unknown. How could they think their efforts would be successful? What made them think they could do any of the remarkable things they did? It had to be Jesus' statement of authority that never stopped ringing in their ears. They knew who He was, what He had done, and what He'd been given. And they believed His promise to be their traveling companion regardless of their GPS location. Just ordinary guys . . . but not so ordinary anymore.

That's the life we've been called to as well. Like the days when Gideon, Samson, Jeremiah, and Simon Peter lived larger than themselves, God has a huge mission for us and He will demonstrate His unlimited capacity through our lives in order to get the job done.

In the Bible, this amazing journey is what we call the Spirit-empowered life.

THINK ABOUT IT

1. How does knowing that Jesus has been given complete authority affect your confidence in Him and His promises?
2. How do you feel knowing He has extended that power to you? Do you want that power?

CHAPTER 5

Are We Close?

I s the life we want the life we've got? Have you ever wondered if the way you live the journey of a Christ-follower matches Jesus' real intent? Now I don't mean to question the numerous stories of power and life change that jump from the pages of church magazines and reports of world missions. But when you think about your own life of faith, does it seem like something's missing?

Jesus' statement of authority and promise of power paint an expectation that's beyond what many Christians experience. It's hard to imagine the apostles yawning their way through local church gatherings, checking the "sundials" on their wrists, and thinking about lunch. Did they crawl over one another on the ladder of spiritual hierarchy, hoping this week's attendance might top last week's crowd, or at least beat the rival worship gathering down the street? While amazing stories pile up in overseas settings, it seems Christianity in our corner of the world has drifted from the power and influence it once held.

If surveys are any indication, most church folks have yet to engage the life-changing impact described by Jesus and preached by the apostles. In recent years, we've discovered little difference between the behavioral choices of those in a church pew and those who spend Sunday mornings mowing their yards. Even in the decisions spoken of most clearly in the Bible—avoiding immorality, abandoning self-centeredness, and preferring godliness to financial abundance—Western Christians show little resolve or self-control. The apostle Paul told us that to be "in Christ" was to be a "new creation" (2 Cor. 5:17), but it seems there's not much new for quite a few believers.

Even for many Pentecostal Christians, those who place a high priority on the Spirit-empowered life, the evidence of such powerful living is lacking. In the first century, just over 100 people full of God's Spirit launched a world-changing mission, but today even larger congregations struggle to exercise much of that power and influence when they leave the church property.

Power marked the revival in Samaria. Even those who practiced dark arts could see the superiority of the impact made by those early disciples. One guy wanted to buy what he saw and quickly learned he was dealing with bigger things than he realized (Acts 8:9–24). A few other guys thought they had the language figured out, but they discovered there was more to this powerful life than a few magic words (19:13–16). At one point, even the sweat rags tossed aside by the apostle Paul proved to have healing capacity (19:12). When was the last time you saw something like that?

Now don't get me wrong. There's much to enjoy in many of America's churches. Today's musicians pound out exhilarating anthems, and in some places people engage in them with rock-concert intensity. Elsewhere, local ponds and portable swimming pools teem with baptism applicants who are cheered amidst palpable celebrations. For some, the ranks of the converted swell with a host of new hands every Sunday. People walk into the local church with a myriad of problems, emerging an hour later with new hope, tear-stained cheeks, and a complimentary Bible.

> Churches today are larger than ever before, but their influence in our culture continues to diminish.

Yet something seems to be missing. Community problems mount and the influence of even the best local church seems to be diminishing. Even within the sacred family, those with life-controlling problems gather in small groups that probably need to be larger. Brokenness is no longer limited to Saturday night's bar scene; instead, it's increasingly evident among even the most faithful. In fact, many churches have rewritten their standards of righteousness since the answers they've been offering struggle to generate real life change.

I don't mean to paint a bleak picture, but the fact remains: though churches today are larger than ever before, their influence in our culture continues to diminish. In some places, pastors can achieve community celebrity, yet their words fall on ears determined to be deaf. How is it that a Spirit-empowered deacon and a few friends brought a culture-altering revival to the community of half-Jews in Samaria, but a half dozen churches containing a quarter of the local population can't seem to make a real difference in their small town today? Where has all the power gone?

I'm not a church critic, and I'm not trying to shape you into one either. I've spent my life (more than a half century) singing gospel songs and stock-piling sermon notes. I listened to my youth pastor when he tried to curb my adolescent urges and did my best to hold the standard he hoped for. Years later, I cajoled my own group of students toward that same high road. As a pastor and parishioner, I've stood on both sides of the altar, hoping the moment's tearful encounter might translate into new choices for the upcoming week. I've fed the hungry and pot-lucked with the well-fed. I've cradled babies in the church nursery and offered devotional encouragement to the aged in nursing homes. While I can't claim to have done it all, I can assure you I've got my money's worth out of more than 2,700 Sundays—and I have no plans to stop.

It's just that I want more, and I don't think I'm being selfish. I think Jesus wants that, too.

I want to see people who grasp for hope find something more than eternal fire insurance. I want friends who sit amidst the broken shards of failed marriage promises to find a path to restoration and new life. I want those who've been abused and cheated and neglected to have the gaping holes in their hearts filled to overflowing. That's what I want, and since you've read this far, I think you want that, too.

How have so many ended up with a spiritual life that's exercised on Sunday, then tucked in a trunk like a ventriloquist's dummy for the next six days? How did so many end up practicing nominal Christianity, where they wear the label without living the life? How did the term *Christian* become more synonymous with political ideology than with righteous living and life-changing power?

There's one more question that haunts me even more. Why is it that people who seemed furthest from God ran toward Jesus, while those hiding behind self-righteous façades couldn't stand to be near Him? And why is it often just the opposite for us?

People were drawn to Jesus' power and then quickly encountered His amazing love. We struggle with both, don't we? And I don't think that was the plan when He announced His authority, promised His presence, and said that people would know we are His disciples by our love (John 13:35).

I'm intrigued when I see that Jesus entrusted His mission to a few simple folks who didn't understand most of the truths they later wrote about. Their theology was fledgling at best. Their message offered great ideas in their earliest infancy. It would be decades before they had mastered a doctrinal statement and more than a dozen centuries before a regular guy could tuck a Bible under his arm. There was so much they didn't have.

Yet they had something we may be missing.

We have wisdom from scholars across multiple nations and cultures just a keystroke away. We have scope and sequence presentations of biblical truth that guarantee a healthy exposure to every doctrinal ideal. We have technology and travel that can bring the gospel servant face to face with nearly all of earth's inhabitants. We have Bibles on top of Bibles and millions of books that help us unlock the Bible's amazing insights. Our praise songs top our charts and engage worshippers throughout the entire global village. But do we have the power that those early Christ-followers carried with them from Jerusalem to Judea, into Samaria, and to the ends of the earth?

Isn't it time to stop listing reasons why world-changing revivals are sweeping the Third World and start chasing some of that ourselves? When will we stop thinking we're on the right track when that track keeps lumbering through boredom and powerless living? When will we become dissatisfied with self-help ideas couched in religious language or ear-tickling promises of heaven on earth for the positive thinkers and visionaries? Jesus came that we might have life, and I'm guessing it looked more like His than ours. That's what I want.

I want a Spirit-empowered life—the kind Jesus died to give me.

THINK ABOUT IT

1. Is your journey with Christ currently in growth mode, or do you feel stalled in your relationship with Him?
2. Do you think God wants us to live powerful lives? If so, why do so many of us live something less?
3. Take a few moments and jot down a few thoughts describing your own idea of a powerful life.

CHAPTER 6

The Transformation

Simon Peter may be the most entertaining of the disciples, and the one who gives the rest of us the most hope. While his forceful personality occasionally lifted him above the rest, his rather frequent missteps somehow kept knocking him down. Whether or not he was the greatest among the original Twelve is up for debate, but clearly he was Jesus' most high-maintenance challenge.

Peter rocked the house with his assertion that Jesus was "the Messiah, the Son of the living God" (Matt. 16:16). His response to Jesus' mid-term exam question, "Who do you say that I am?" would have received a "10" even from the Eastern European judge. And we can applaud him for jumping out of the boat when given the opportunity to stroll with Jesus on the waves (14:28–29). Sure, he came up a bit short before that story ends, but none of the others were drying their feet that night.

But if his high points scraped a ceiling the others never approached, his low points found a barrel's bottom like no other, too.

The most stunning of Peter's failures occurred in the worst possible moment. Sitting around their final Passover table, Jesus alluded to His nearing betrayal (Mark 14:18). Apparently, Jesus knew that the religious leaders wouldn't make their move until one of His own guys turned on Him. Such news couldn't have been easy for the Twelve to hear, but rather than respond with a willing anger to kill whoever would do such a thing, Peter timidly suggested, "Ask him which one he means" (John 13:24).

Was that all their three years of learning and doing had produced? After all they'd seen and done, how could they feel so weak in the moment their Savior might really need them?

Later that night, perhaps to prove his mettle, Peter greeted the approaching soldiers and high priest's servants with flashing steel. One swing severed an ear from the head of the one perhaps standing closest. It's hard to figure why that blow wasn't meant for Judas, but either way, Peter's action brought a swift rebuke from the One he was trying to protect (John 18:10–12). Apparently, after three years of learning and doing, there was still a lot Peter didn't understand.

His sword stayed in its sheath the rest of the night, but his failures were only getting started. As he and John followed the arresting party, anxious to see where they might take Jesus, their heart rates had to be mounting. At the high priest's door, John entered, but Peter remained outside until a servant girl was instructed to let him enter. Apparently, as she escorted him into the house, she asked, "You aren't one of this man's disciples too, are you?" (John 18:17). We can forgive her use of the double negative as servants weren't likely given much education, but how can we understand Peter's response?

"I am not."

Really? Peter, you knelt in your own boat with an overwhelming catch of fish lapping against your knees when you first realized who Jesus was. You watched fish and bread multiply in the basket you carried among a massive crowd. You saw focus return to the eyes of the blind and sanity re-emerge in the lives of the demon-possessed. You walked on water, even if only for a few feet, and fell on your face when Jesus met Moses and Elijah on the mountaintop. Now you want to hide all that from a servant girl who already knows the answer to her question? And she's letting you catch up to John, whom everyone in the house knows is a disciple of Jesus.

Really?

Once in the courtyard, Peter found a fire to warm himself and the question came again. I'm sure it was hard to see the faces in the darkness, so perhaps this was a scarier lot, but after you've melted before a servant girl, every crowd looks like a brewing mob. Same question, same answer. It seems the closer Peter's feet drew to Jesus that night, the further his heart drifted away.

Finally, a third opportunity arose. This time, the question came from a relative of the fella who had temporarily lost his ear to Peter's sword earlier that evening. Now this guy could be a problem. Once again Peter denied any connection to what he had done and to the One he had tried to do it for.

Right on cue, a distant rooster sounded the first break of daylight. The startling sound shook Peter violently as he realized that in one night he had thrown away the great future he'd been dreaming of only a few hours before.

That should have been the end of the line for Simon Peter, don't you think? If you can't get more out of a three-year opportunity to live in Jesus' actual shadow, I'd say it's time to give someone else a chance. It seems like there should have been an angel with a clipboard somewhere shouting, "Next!"

But miraculously, no one slammed an eternal door on Simon Peter that tragic night. Instead, after His own lonely and gruesome death, Jesus reappeared and restored the troubled fisherman. That's why we like this bumbling disciple—his story gives hope to the rest of us bumblers.

Weeks later, the scene has shifted dramatically. Jesus has passed the baton of His amazing mission to those who had followed Him and then He disappeared into a cloud. Uncertain what to do, the disciples made Matthias an official member of their group (to replace the betrayer, Judas Iscariot, and return their number to twelve) and then huddled together in a room, waiting for Jesus to return with a plan, a kingdom, or some idea of next steps. He had told them to wait for something (a command we'll consider more deeply in the next chapter), so wait they did.

As Jerusalem buzzed with the concluding celebration of firstfruits (a feast remembering the giving of the law and the launching of Judaism), suddenly the room became like fire. Words were inadequate to describe the moment, but it felt like a wind was shaking the stone walls around them. Something . . . no, Someone . . . a Presence lifted them from the inside and strange syllables raced from their hearts to their mouths, creating a majestic cacophony of the unknown (Acts 2:1–4).

Crowds quickly gathered as Jews from distant places heard voices praising God in the languages of home. What was happening? How could simple Galileans like these know how to speak these languages?

These unknown "tongues" were coming from the Spirit of God as He filled each person in that remarkable room.

How indeed? In verse 4, the Greek word translated "enabled them" is αποθεγγομαι (pronounced apo-theng-o-my), and it means Spirit-inspired speech. In other words, these unknown "tongues" were coming from the Spirit of God as He filled each person in that remarkable room.

Once the moment subsided and those inside regained their emotional bearings, the crowd's questions needed to be answered. But, who should speak?

Now I would have voted for John. Even though he was the youngest of the disciples, he had been the most loyal to Jesus during His trial and crucifixion and was the first to race to the tomb. John would ultimately be a primary voice throughout the first century of the church, teaching Jesus' message of love with laudable clarity. As the questions mounted, and some of the crowd were thinking the group was drunk, my eyes are on John.

Instead, Simon Peter stepped forward. Oh great! No matter how many mistakes the guy made, he was never afraid to make another!

But something had changed. Simon Peter, the guy who couldn't find his voice in front of a servant girl, began to speak with a clarity and power that knew no fear. He was not afraid to be seen as the leader of this puzzling disturbance. He stepped up to connect the historical dots to ancient prophecies and to connect the crowd to their responsibility for Jesus' death. Wow! Talk about an altar call that gets into your business! "Jesus, whom you crucified" (Acts 2:36) he shouted, as if he wanted his words to get back to the high priest that instant.

What a difference! What had happened to the fearful bumbler? As Luke tells this story, he lets us in on the transformation by using that same word, αποθεγγομαι, when describing Peter's speech (v. 14). Peter's words were flowing from the same Source that had brought the unknown languages. His words were Spirit-empowered, and from that moment forward, so would be his life.

We call this moment "Pentecost," a name that connects to the Jewish feast that day but means so much more today. This was the launching moment of the church, the outpouring of God's Spirit on Jesus' little band, and the launching of the mission He had given to them. This is the picture of a Spirit-empowered life, perhaps never seen more clearly in the Bible than in the life of Simon Peter.

A few days after this experience, Peter grabbed a lame man by the hand and lifted him to his suddenly healed feet. Later, Peter was dragged into prison but spoke with such wisdom and understanding that he blew the minds of the religious leaders. He escaped from that prison, the recipient of an angel rescue, and became the leader he was meant to be for the Jerusalem church. Before long, Peter was at a Roman centurion's house when salvation and the Spirit-empowered life first came to a Gentile.

He was Simon Peter . . . wait, make that Spirit-empowered Simon Peter, who had become the rock Jesus always knew he could be (Matt. 16:18).

THINK ABOUT IT

1. Do you think Peter's transformation was more than just renewed self-discipline and determination? Explain your answer.
2. In what ways has God already transformed your life?

CHAPTER 7

Staying Put

H ave you ever wondered what Jesus was thinking when He heard that distant rooster sound the morning alarm? You know, the moment He knew Peter would be kicking himself for being so weak? I suppose Jesus could have thought, *Told you so*, like someone who was fed up with Peter's regular efforts to get attention. *That ought to shut you up for awhile!*

Of course, we know that wasn't Jesus' attitude.

Perhaps He felt sorry for Peter and wondered how the impetuous disciple would fare over the next few days as he dealt with what he had done. When Jesus warned that Peter would deny Him, Jesus told the fisherman that Satan wanted to "sift all of you as wheat" but that Jesus had prayed for them (Luke 22:31–32). That probably tells us what Jesus felt—He had compassion for His friend and the painful self-discovery Peter faced that night.

The fact is, Jesus knows our weaknesses, doesn't He? Yet He doesn't use that knowledge to poke fun at us or magnify our inability to be everything we boast of being. Today, He doesn't sit on that heavenly throne celebrating when we get our comeuppance. Instead, the writer of Hebrews says that He is moved by our weaknesses (Heb. 4:15).

Jesus knew Peter would fail because He knew that Peter wasn't ready for the overwhelming emotion of that enormous night. He knew because Peter didn't yet have the strength within him or the power of God's Spirit to face the onslaught of God's eternal enemy.

In fact, as Jesus thought of each of the disciples that night, He must have wondered at their capacity. Would they be able to face the life ahead without Him? They couldn't possibly understand that the road of suffering Jesus traversed would eventually claim them as well. Sure, Jesus' mind could have been solely on His own painful moments of physical beating and unjust treatment, but something tells me His thoughts drifted toward the "little ones" who had followed Him.

He had tried to tell them that "no servant is greater than his master"

(John 13:16). He knew that those who hated Him would come to hate them as well. For each of the men who called Him Lord, life would be difficult and would demand the ultimate sacrifice. At the first taste of that, Peter had stumbled badly because he wasn't ready—none of them were.

That's why Jesus' prayer for them was "Father, protect them" (17:11). I might expect Him to ask God to equip them, empower them, or make them great. That's what I want Jesus to pray for me. Instead, He spoke like a field general worried about the future of His men. "Keep them, hold them together, let them be one," . . . what did Jesus know that they didn't?

Jesus knew that what He was asking of them was bigger than any dream they'd ever considered. These guys were local boys. In fact, their strolls with Jesus across the Judean countryside were likely as far from home as many had ever been. These guys were going to board ships and sail to distant lands where they would infiltrate non-Jewish cultures with a message foreign to the sensibilities of all who heard. That's quite a thought, isn't it?

> Jesus knew that what He was asking of them was bigger than any dream they'd ever considered.

When you read the book of Acts, you see the racist ideas many of the apostles held. They believed the Jews were superior and possessed sole access to God. Others could gather the crumbs that fell from Jewish tables, but the real stuff was for their countrymen (Matt. 15:27). Doesn't sound like your typical missionary mentality, does it? How were they going to get past such ideas?

And education hadn't been their ticket to new thinking either. Most of these men were from among the lower classes where they'd likely learned more at home than school, provided their parents had been diligent to teach them. Their advanced learning wouldn't be opening many doors because they couldn't reach that kind of doorknob.

So how were these men going to fulfill this Commission? Now, I'm sure Jesus had great confidence in the Father's plan, but when He was the "boots on the ground" and had looked into those confused eyes day after day, there had to be a little uncertainty. Clearly, these men were going to need help—supernatural help—if they were going to fulfill a worldwide strategy.

So Jesus told them to wait.

Now, we can get pretty excited about the Great Commission. Perhaps only John 3:16 has been fodder for more sermons than Jesus' "Go" command at the end of each Synoptic Gospel. And when Acts 1:8 distributes our directional orders—Jerusalem, Judea, Samaria, and the ends of the earth—well, we're ready to go! Everyone put a hand in here and on three . . . !

But just before He told us we would be His witnesses in places near and far, Jesus said, "Wait." Here's the actual statement:

> On one occasion, while he was eating with them, he gave them this command: "Do not leave Jerusalem, but wait for the gift my Father promised, which you have heard me speak about. For John baptized with water, but in a few days you will be baptized with the Holy Spirit." (Acts 1:4–5)

Wait! How did we miss that?

Perhaps like Simon Peter on that night in Gethsemane, we're anxious to be people of action. We're ready to do something, swords drawn. Let's show Jesus what we're made of!

But Jesus said, "Wait."

Why? Because He knew our weakness, He knew the road ahead of us, He knew the size of the task we'd been given and the Enemy who would block our paths. He knew we weren't nearly as ready as we thought we were, and that once trouble arose, we'd drop those swords and run as fast as Peter did that fateful night. He knew we'd need more than our collective willpower and enthusiasm, because this battle is bigger than we are.

So He said "Wait," and He had something specific in mind. "Wait for the gift my Father promised, which you have heard me speak about . . . you will be baptized with the Holy Spirit."

Now we've already seen what that Pentecost moment did to transform Simon Peter. In one remarkable prayer meeting, he went from an unstable fisherman riding the waves of his own emotions to a rock God could use to build His amazing kingdom. And Peter wasn't the only one. Jesus had extraordinary plans for each of the 120 who filled the upper room that day. And each of them would need the same kind of transforming moment to launch them toward the Spirit-empowered life He intended them to live.

You may think, *Sure, that's a great story, but it's tucked tightly into the world of then and them. What does it have to do with me?*

Does this story have application for those of us who read it from a distance of nearly two millennia? Put more simply, can we expect to experience the same?

Many have argued the issue of whether or not a Spirit-empowered moment is "normative" for all Christians. In other words, was this simply the catalyzing of a few early believers, or does God want every Christian to encounter that same "baptism"?

Well, let's first consider what happened next for them. After Acts 1:4–5 was fulfilled for the first time in Acts 2:1–4, the church got off to a roaring start. Three thousand converted on day one. I'll bet you'd have serious parking problems if your local church had a day like that!

But a few chapters later, persecution was accelerating, and the believers recognized their lack of strength to face such threats. Peter and John had already been imprisoned for healing a lame man in the name of their recently executed leader (Jesus). Though they were released, it wasn't without some pretty clear threats. So the local group of disciples begged God to help them, to give them boldness to keep moving forward with the mission. Here's what happened next as they prayed:

> We're only through ten chapters in the book of Acts, following just one thread of the gospel's spread, and it's already clear that the Acts 2 experience wasn't just a one-time thing.

> "Indeed Herod and Pontius Pilate met together with the Gentiles and the people of Israel in this city to conspire against your holy servant Jesus, whom you anointed. They did what your power and will had decided beforehand should happen. Now, Lord, consider their threats and enable your servants to speak your word with great boldness. Stretch out your hand to heal and perform signs and wonders through the name of your holy servant Jesus."
>
> After they prayed, the place where they were meeting was shaken. And they were all filled with the Holy Spirit and spoke the word of God boldly. (Acts 4:27–31)

Did you catch that last line? "They were all filled with the Holy Spirit." That's the same phrase that described the initial outpouring in Acts 2:4, isn't it?

In fact, such moments kept happening.

Saul of Tarsus (later called Paul) experienced his empowering in Acts 9:17. Next, this Spirit-baptism fell on a Roman centurion and his household, much to the surprise of the apostle who thought God only wanted to dwell among the Jews (10:45–46). We're only through ten chapters in the book of Acts, following just one thread of the gospel's spread, and it's already clear that the Acts 2 experience wasn't just a one-time thing.

It became an expected thing.

When "revival" hit Samaria through Philip's preaching, the apostles in Jerusalem sent Peter and John to check things out. They didn't make that northward trek to shut down the spread of the gospel to this somewhat despised region. They went to introduce these new converts to the power of the Holy Spirit. Luke's account makes it clear that the priority of this promise served as the sole motive for the mission (8:14–17). Jesus knew His own disciples would need the power of the Spirit to fulfill the mission, and now His disciples learned that even Samaritans would need that same power.

Consider that there may be no Bible moment more clearly revealing of the early church's understanding of Spirit-empowerment than when the apostle Paul happened upon a band of believers from Ephesus. Here, Paul's first question for the gathering of the believers was, "Did you receive the Holy Spirit when you believed?" (19:1–2). That question tells us a lot.

These early followers of Jesus understood the importance of receiving the power of the Holy Spirit. It was Paul's first question, and it's the only part of their conversation that Luke shares with us. Why? Because Jesus said "Wait!" and His followers took that to mean priority. To live a Spirit-empowered life and to pursue the amazing path God has designed for our lives, we too must wait for a power greater than our own.

For the Christ-followers of the early church, Spirit-empowerment meant clear direction, unstudied knowledge and wisdom, remarkable endurance, and miracle-working power when the situation demanded. Doesn't that sound like the same list we bring to God as we serve His mission? You and I can't manufacture such things, and when we try, we're left with our own inadequacies and a short path to failure.

Jesus sees the same hunger in us, but He also sees our weaknesses, the road ahead of us, the size of our task, and the Enemy who seeks to shut us down. Does it make sense to think we can handle this on our own? That's unlikely, isn't it? And, that's why the Spirit-empowered life must be as important and available to us as it was to them.

Bottom line? I want His life of more—and Jesus knows I need it.

THINK ABOUT IT

1. Why might it have been difficult for those early disciples to obey Jesus' command to wait?
2. Have you experienced a moment like theirs, when God fulfilled His promise of power in your life?

CHAPTER 8

Gotta Have More

I n the past few chapters, we've seen the biblical evidence for more. The transformation I came to Jesus to find demands something greater than I can achieve through my learning and doing. Think about what that means for a moment.

I can't change myself.

Isn't that what we admitted when we first came to Jesus in need of hope, cleansing, and life change? We settled that in our minds, and when we heard that God was "in town" we came "running." If we had the capacity to change our own direction, to be free from the life patterns we had established, and to walk a path toward greater fulfillment and peace, well, wouldn't we have been doing that? God wasn't our shortcut to a path we could find on our own. He and His mercy were the *only* path to get there.

I can change a few habits, but even that proves difficult. I might decide to stop eating certain foods that fill the unhealthy list, but that usually maxes out my willpower. A gym membership or the purchase of a treadmill can help me learn to prioritize exercise, but that's a habit that's easy to break for some reason. So after a while, the treadmill gets pushed farther into the corner where it can be covered with a blanket.

If there's going to be cataclysmic change in my life, I have no problem admitting I need help because I don't have what I need to make that happen. Now, I'm not going to say that God has to do all the work, but He's going to have to be involved significantly and provide both the possibility and the power for me to become someone different.

By nature, I'm a quiet guy. Ask my wife. She'll tell you that I can ride silently in the car for hours, something she occasionally finds frustrating. When a need arises, I'm glad to help, but I don't step into such moments with a great deal of force. I don't start conversations comfortably, and there are many times I'd like to be better at sharing my faith with the guy in the next airplane seat. It's just that it's hard to be that guy. Sometimes I wish I were more aggressive and, honestly, sometimes the situation demands it. In fact, if I'm going to live a Spirit-empowered life, I think that would be a part of what it would look like.

I think I might be a lot like Bartholomew—you know, one of the disciples we don't know much about. Sometimes he's called Nathanael and about all we hear of him was when Jesus first found him. Jesus immediately saw that Bart was honest and sincere. "No deceit" is the tag (John 1:47). But once he joined Jesus' merry band, he didn't get his name in the story much. He was not loud like Simon Peter, and he didn't have a past like Matthew. He had no apparent family among the disciples like James and John, nor did he have a political agenda like Simon the Zealot. He was just a good guy, and I wish I knew more about what Acts 2:4 helped him become, because I think I'd want some of the same.

Of course, we're all different, aren't we?

You might be like Simon Peter—kind of "out there" with your opinions and emotions. Honestly, people like you make me a little nervous, but you're fun to have around. I admire your ability to embrace life with both hands (a leg, and the occasional elbow). When you enter a room, the atmosphere changes. People want to be around you, to swim in the wake you create. They say you're a "natural" leader, and I know that whatever you do tends to be big, even if it doesn't always turn out like you hoped.

For Peter, the need was stability and firmness. That's the whole idea behind the "rock" label Jesus gave him. But being Spirit-empowered meant even more than that for the fisherman. It meant maximizing his boldness, even giving him the courage to proclaim healing for a lame man and to bring life to a dead woman. Spirit-empowered living took the best of Peter's capacity to a whole new level while injecting some new strength into his weak areas. Doesn't that sound like something you need?

Perhaps John is more your speed. He was the youngest of the disciples, perhaps a late teen when the journey with Jesus began. But there was no back seat on the bus for this kid. John was right in the middle of everything Jesus did. Maybe

> **Spirit-empowered living took the best of Peter's capacity to a whole new level while injecting some new strength into his weak areas.**

his brother's stature opened the door, but John was a genuine learner. He made his mistakes but was willing to accept correction. He was the guy Jesus could always count on, the one who would stand unashamedly at the cross with Jesus' mother while the other guys were hiding in the crowd.

When I think of John, the word *dependable* comes to mind. Is that you? Perhaps you're the one everybody counts on to get the job done. You may not demand the most attention, but you're always there, ready and willing to take on any challenge. You see every day as a chance to learn a little more or be a bit better at everything you think or do.

The Spirit-empowered John became known as the "apostle of love." Now, that wasn't a moniker that described sensual love or careless sexual behavior. Instead, it was a testimony to the fact that John grasped the main idea of Jesus' teaching. John's the one who put the premium on love. He connected the dots between what Jesus did and how the Father loves. He's the one who insisted we must love in order for people to connect us to Jesus. Don't believe me? Read his first epistle (1 John), and you'll encounter the treatise of this disciple's life.

Matthew was another story, maybe one like yours. While each of the disciples had a less than satisfying life before meeting Jesus, Matthew's was more of a mess. Some of the story is told in his occupation. Matthew was a tax collector—a Jew who worked with the Romans to extort as much money as possible out of his countrymen. Tax collectors served the oppressors and often lined their own pockets with any additional funds they might get.

We grasp even more of Matthew's story from the dinner he gave in Jesus' honor. He invited his friends, and religious folks turned up their noses at the scene (Mark 2:15–16). He was one of "those kind of people" when Jesus entered his life. Of course, "those kind of people" showed up often in Jesus' story, and the results were pretty special.

> No one's a more passionate rescuer than the one who knows what it feels like to be drowning.

Do you connect with Matthew? Sure, your story is different, but maybe you number among the millions who have found Jesus after a journey of tragic choices. You like Matthew because he ran after Jesus the way you did and, well, you understand the limp in his gait. What does a Spirit-empowered

Matthew look like? He's a world-changer with a powerful story to tell to the most-broken people. In fact, in stories like Matthew's, Jesus takes the pieces of what used to be destructive and turns those exact pieces into a meaningful and productive life. No one's a more passionate rescuer than the one who knows what it feels like to be drowning.

Of course, Thomas was a different guy altogether. Some would call him melancholy or one with deep emotions. I think of him as an "all in" kind of guy. He was stubborn and could frustrate you when he didn't want to go your way, but when he was with you, well, he wasn't turning back.

His name lands in the gospel story in two very important places. The second made him famous, though I'm not sure we treat him fairly. We call him "Doubting Thomas," but I think "Desperate Thomas" might be more fair. As you probably know, Thomas missed the first gathering where Jesus appeared to the disciples after His resurrection, and he wasn't ready to believe that the guys had seen Jesus. Thomas had seen Jesus die and watched his own hope die with Him. How could Jesus be alive again? Thomas wasn't ready to believe so soon after his own hopes had been crushed. Of course, he didn't miss the second meeting, and church history tells us that once Thomas was full of the Holy Spirit, nothing ever stopped him again.

The first time we hear from Thomas in Jesus' story was months earlier, when Jesus turned toward Jerusalem for what would prove to be the final time. Each of the disciples knew what another visit to the neighborhood of the religious leaders would bring, but it was Thomas who said, "Let us also go, that we may die with him" (John 11:16). Wow! Now that's a guy I want on my side!

Is that you? Do you feel things deeply? People with passion are powerful allies, no matter the challenge. But sometimes such people can become discouraged, especially when the people they're counting on seem to have failed. People like Thomas can't just shrug off such disappointment but tend to carry it with them longer than most. Think what the power of the Holy Spirit can do to magnify that passion and heal those hurts. Lots of Thomases have done amazing things for God in every generation.

So which person are you? Sure, we didn't get to Andrew, James, or the rest of the guys in the traveling party. But the point is that they, like us, had their own unique personalities and their own specially designed purposes. No two disciples are exactly alike. That's a demonstration of the immense creativity of the One who has made us. You're a unique collection of traits and experiences, and God enjoys bringing out your best with the power of His Spirit.

That's what the Spirit-empowered life will do. There's no cookie-cutter model that God wants you to become. You're not designed to be a superior or inferior version of someone else. Instead, He wants to maximize your greatest strengths and solidify those areas that used to hold you back. You are one of the billions of unique expressions from the mind of your Creator, and He wants to fill your life and shape you into the greatest version of you that can be found.

Do you want that? I do.

That's what I mean when I say, *I want more.* I want more of my best and more strength to conquer my worst. I want to live the life I was made for. As the apostle Paul put it, I want to "take hold of that for which Christ Jesus took hold of me" (Phil. 3:12).

You see, the first step toward the Spirit-empowered life is to want such a life, even to know you need it. When Jesus laid His Commission before the disciples, they each had a choice. They could walk away and pursue their own agendas; they could go back to fishing or collecting taxes. Or they could live the journey Jesus had invited them to engage. Judas bailed, but the rest of the guys said, "We want more!"

Do you want more?

In these eight chapters, I've tried to shape that question in your mind, but at some point you have to answer it. The pages that follow will help you pursue and ultimately express that life, but they have no value until you choose. I can't keep you from reading on to see what's involved before you make up your mind, but remember that Jesus asked His disciples to follow before they knew where the road might lead. I can tell you that God has a road uniquely designed for you to walk, and He has promised to walk that road with you.

For me, that's enough to start chasing the Spirit-empowered life!

THINK ABOUT IT

1. What strengths do you possess, and what would they look like if maximized by God's power?
2. What weaknesses have you never thought you'd overcome?

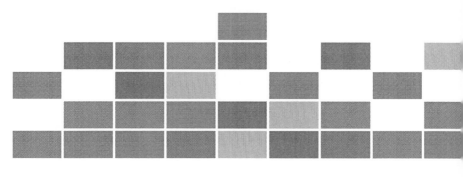

THE ENCOUNTER

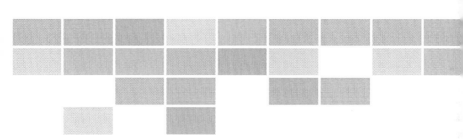

CHAPTER 9

Relationship: More Than Believing

L
ike most people, I enjoy watching the Olympics. I love the way athleticism and patriotism blend to get me cheering for people I had previously never heard of, and then goad me into celebrating their successes with an exuberant, "We did it!" Of course, those who win will be "heard of" again and again, even if they never realized that I was on their side.

In my opinion, the most compelling of the Olympic events is the 100-meter dash. That's the race where we crown the "world's fastest human" (assuming each country actually found its fastest guy). It's hard to think that some fella might be sitting in his living room, remote in hand, with the ability to outrun the guy he's cheering for.

I'm not that guy. I made the high school track team as a distance runner—not because of the size of my stride but because of the size of my school. Still, I know a bit about those speed races. I know the start is critical, but it's not the whole race.

Each runner calibrates his metal starting blocks, laces his shoes tightly, and stretches every leg and shoulder muscle as he prepares to take his mark. He then crouches into position, coiling himself up as tightly as a NASA rocket just before blast off. Then, he tries to time his launch perfectly, hoping to burst from the blocks the very millisecond the gun fires its empty chamber toward the sky. If he's a moment too early, he can be disqualified. If he's a moment late, he may not be able to catch the other runners. You can't win the race in the starting blocks, but they say you sure can lose it there.

The start is critical . . . but it's not the race.

The race is what happens after the gun sounds. It's what happens after the runners rise from that explosive crouch and demonstrate their superior speed. The race is what happens when those long, powerful legs stride to cover the maximum inches of track, and ankles recoil and propel at their most intense rate. The race is every amazing moment that unfolds until the runners thrust their chests forward in hopes of touching the tape just ahead of their competitors. And it's there that someone wins the race and takes a glory lap in celebration.

Following Christ is more than just the start as well, but I'm afraid there are times when many would-be "runners" and those who "coach" them have confused the starting line with the race. In this modern era of the Western church, great focus is given to Christianity's starting line—we call it "a decision." Great Sunday services are capped with these decisions, hands are lifted and feet move toward the front of the auditorium. The awareness of God's love and a desire to feel His embrace are truly appealing, so people by the dozens overcome their fear of public display and walk those aisles to be added to the local number of disciples.

It's a great start, but it's not the race.

Let's take a minute to consider that start. How amazing is it that God loves us? Seriously, what reason can we give Him to do so? In spite of the creative genius He invested in our very being, we live for ourselves, chasing short-term satisfaction and never bothering to consider how we got here and what the One who put us here might want. We do our own thing until one day we discover that God has a thing. Usually, we realize that only when our things have stopped working. So we stand with hat in hand hoping the eternal Judge will find some mercy in His briefcase—and He does!

By mere confession of sin and a genuine desire to turn from its path, a door now opens to us. Like Matthew, we get to jump from our tax collection booth because Jesus wants us to. Matthew's colleague Zacchaeus even had Jesus in his dining room, offering him a life he suddenly wanted desperately. Talk about good news!

There's no doubt that

> The idea that God would open His door to us is remarkable and should bring joy to us every day.

the invitation to salvation tops the chart of human experience. God is willing to wipe our slate clean, to forgive our deepest stupidities. Salvation is the most amazing gift, and God offers it to every one of us, no matter our . . . well, you name it.

The idea that God would open His door to us is remarkable and should bring joy to us every day. Honestly, I don't think anyone can get accustomed to the idea. A few minutes reflecting on the fact that God has come to us still brings tears to my eyes, even fifty years after finding that open door. This gift of God is incredible . . . but it's only the beginning.

On the other side of that door is life! There's a race to run, there's a journey to discover, there's a God-guided future with destinations we could never have found on our own. God has a life—a Spirit-empowered life—just waiting for us.

How can we think the start is all that matters? We count noses at our altars, seeming to imply that the standard's been met, the box has been checked. We can start our own journeys again—clean as a whistle. And that altar will be available next Sunday if our hearts need a touch-up, maybe a buff and a wax. We keep doing our thing and trying to do it better and a little nicer, and God will keep washing us down when we need it. That car-wash existence isn't Christianity—at least not the brand Jesus died to give us!

He opened God's eternal door so we could step into something new. There's a life and a purpose waiting for anyone who responds to His, "Come, follow Me." Salvation is just the door—and an amazing door it is—to a life with God that has no expiration date.

Can you imagine being invited to a friend's house to watch the Olympics or to enjoy a great meal, but you decide to stand in the doorway rather than go inside? Wouldn't that seem awkward? Sure, you knocked and he answered, probably even smiled as he offered, "Come on in."

But you just wanted to stop by, to see if the door was open, and to catch that quick smile before going your own way. Yeah, he's home and yes, you're welcome here, so . . . good to know . . . check the box. Was that the point of your friend's invitation?

No, he wanted you to come in so you could spend time together. He wanted you to eat with him and enjoy a deeper connection. Getting his door open was a good start, but the point of the invitation runs much deeper.

A big part of God's plan is that we would choose the life He has offered. Now what that life looks like proves different for each of us, but there's a common point to each of our choices to enter—it's a life of following Him. We characterize that idea by saying we "give our lives to Him," echoing the apostle Paul's idea of being living sacrifices (Rom. 12:1). It's a life with God in charge, guiding us to fulfill His purposes and doing so to help people see how great He is. We'll talk more about the nature of this life a bit later, but we need to grasp the real nature of God's invitation.

Honestly, I hear a lot of modern preachers describe the starting line without revealing much about the race that follows. They paint comforting pictures of the doorway, describing its beauty, peaceful designs, with a doorknob that's light to the touch. And when we open it, balloons fall, heaven celebrates, and we win a prize package that includes an all-expense paid trip to heaven. Frankly, when I hear many such invitations, I can't imagine why anyone in their right mind would say, "No, thanks." Imagine seeing the Publisher's Clearing House van in your driveway and pretending you're not at home.

Yes, salvation is great news, an amazing gift, and the benefits are off the charts, but some of our descriptions of that door don't mesh easily with Jesus saying that those who would come after Him must first count the cost (Luke 14:28).

Cost? Hey, Pastor, was that in the fine print?

Jesus' full invitation was to more than the door. To follow means to come *after!* It requires letting someone else lead. It insists on letting someone else choose the agenda. Following doesn't mean Jesus fills my tank and waves as I pull away. It clearly implies that He drives, and I have chosen to stay close to His bumper.

Sadly, many people file into churches each week dissatisfied with their experience. They believe the right things and can usually get their Testaments in the right order. They believe, and they learn, and they even do—when they're all doing stuff together—but they don't really live. Somehow they have the idea that the first step was the only step until they take the final step on a golden street.

Spirit-empowered people chase a missional life.

Spirit-empowered people chase a missional life. We embrace each day with a sense of purpose—the one handed to us by the same God who is forming us into something new. We breathe with an awareness of God breathing around us. And we begin finding a life that's more abundant and extraordinary than common language can describe.

I want more, and that means I want to engage every available step that's on the other side of salvation's threshold. And if you're going to live a Spirit-empowered life, that's what you'll be looking for, too. So take a moment every day to reflect on the miracle that first opened that door to you, but don't stop there. Embrace the life God has invited you to live. That's the whole point. That's what it means to engage relationship with God.

That's the real race . . .

THINK ABOUT IT

1. Take a few minutes to remember the day you first believed in Jesus and chose to give Him your life. How might your life be different today if that moment had never occurred?

2. In what way do you think that day was only the beginning? How have you seen a bit of the "more" God may have for your life?

CHAPTER
10

Relationship: This Comes First

The Spirit-empowered life starts with relationship. To pursue the Spirit-empowered life, there can be only one starting point—a relational connection with God Himself. This is the unexpected mystery of God's activity among the people He created—He wants to lead us, live among us, and have relationship with us. A bit later, we'll reflect on the implications of this stunning mystery, but we must start with this revealed truth as simple fact. God wants us to know Him!

To pursue the Spirit-empowered life, there are two essential steps: (1) relationship and (2) experience. That's not too surprising since every connection we make with others is built from such material. We encounter one another, and we share experiences where our paths merge. The result is friendship—life with one another. And when one party to such a connection is God, well, things should get pretty amazing.

Where many believers miss this life, however, is when they replace the idea of relationship with standards, facts, or behaviors. To these people, the Christian life is something to achieve, and it ultimately becomes little more than a religious system they adhere to. For them, knowing God sounds too subjective, touchy-feely, or like an activity for the next life. For the present, they just need to think the right stuff and do some good stuff—that's Christianity, right?

Jesus showed us something different.

After centuries of having a list of God's standards for living—and proving such a list fails to produce real heart change—we suddenly see God Himself cooing at surprised animals in an innkeeper's barn. They'd never seen anything like that in their feeding trough, and human history shared their surprise. God was now with us? Wow!

For the next thirty-plus years, Jesus lived among us—God in the flesh—

not so we could get the facts straight about God or see His steely determination when commanding us to obey, but so we could *know* Him. He was flesh and blood, handshakes and hugs, warm eyes, kind smile, and probably a beard (as if that could make Him look wiser). Jesus came to achieve many things, but surely the top priority was to prove that God didn't just want to make rules. He wanted us to know Him.

That's why the life God intends for us goes beyond acknowledging Him and being confident that the events of the first Good Friday provided what we need to go to heaven. God wasn't just establishing the right religious system. He said things like "remain in me" (John 15:4), "follow me" (Mark 2:14), and even "keep watch with me" (Matt. 26:40). He was the Bread of Life who took time to eat breakfast with real folks (John 21:9)—and lunch and dinner, too.

Jesus showed God's intent was relationship—a personal connection that couldn't help but transform us and send us on a higher path than we could previously have known. And it's in that relationship where everything starts for us. Jesus described it as being "born again" when talking to a guy who was looking for the right system (John 3:3). Jesus didn't merely want to fix Nicodemus's thinking on various issues—no easy task with religious leaders, either then or now—He wanted to give him a new life, where God would fill him and lead him to so much more.

When we read about Jesus, it's hard not to like Him. The Gospels describe Him as an attraction to increasing throngs of people. Even people who seemed a million miles from the standards righteous people adhere to wanted to get close to Jesus. Somehow the rules made God seem distant, but the way Jesus lived brought Him surprisingly close.

> Somehow the rules made God seem distant, but the way Jesus lived brought Him surprisingly close.

Can we know God? What would that look like?

Some people settle for knowing about God. They pursue learning about God as a class project to master or a slate of ideas to affirm. Many efforts to "make disciples" focus heavily on content download, like a school that never ends. Graduations are celebrated at cemeteries, where coffins and suits serve as caps and gowns. They learn all they can, mastering the Master's content—the apparent path to pleasing God that so many try to take.

Now, knowing about God surely matters, but knowing *Him* sounds more amazing, doesn't it? There's such a difference! Would you rather read a biography or make a friend? I'm a big fan of Abraham Lincoln, but I'd trade every book I've ever read about our sixteenth president for an hour chatting with him over coffee. No, I'm not crazy enough to think that could actually happen, but I actually *can* chat with God! That's the whole point, minus perhaps the coffee.

I'm certainly not against learning, for wisdom is often a product of knowledge. But relationship is a much more pleasing goal. And those who practice learning as the end in itself tend to become more focused on their superior understanding than they are on the One they claim to understand. Those who seek to learn often become proud of their learning and are only too happy to prove how much they've learned or how much more they've learned than you or I. Surely that's not God's real endgame.

It seems odd to me that God would have learning as the primary goal and then hand off His kingdom to a handful of uneducated fishermen. Wouldn't gathering the most excellent teachers have been a better way of reaching such a goal? He needed people who could get the job done, not a bunch of characters who had a long way to grow. Honestly, when we read the Gospel accounts closely, it's hard to tell just how much the disciples had learned after nearly three years of round-the-clock study.

Doing is a similar trap. For some, Christianity is simply about doing good things. Compare the number of good items on our list before becoming Christians to the number of such checkmarks afterward and we should see a marked increase. Christians are do-gooders, and well, there's a lot of good that needs to get done.

Now, I'm not against doing good either. I think it's important when each generation of the church awakens to its responsibility to address social needs, share resources with the lacking, and make a dent in the darker conduct of their cultures. I still have a WWJD bracelet somewhere and think that its mandate is one of the best patterns for living. I'm a doer, and I think Jesus would want me to be one.

But doing has to flow from relationship. It can't be the end in itself. When everything's about doing, we discover that we can't do enough, and we run out of steam pretty quickly. Church calendars are packed with doing opportunities, sometimes to give us a chance to stretch our spiritual legs and build some real life-changing muscle, and sometimes because there's just so much to do. So we do and do and do and do. And long before we get to the end of all that doing, we're weary, depleted, and fed up with those who won't do for themselves. I've met a lot of doers who have stopped doing altogether because that road seemed to always be taking from them. Some of them have pretty sour attitudes now, with faces that don't smile like Jesus did.

The apostle Paul warned us about putting too much confidence in our doing. He reminded us that our works don't provide our real hope (Eph. 2:8–9) and that even on our best days, our best efforts will never meet God's standard (Rom. 6:19). Paul wasn't trying to put an end to bake sales for missionary needs or buying coffee at the drive-thru for the car behind us. He just didn't want us to think that our good deeds were God's primary goal.

Learning and doing aren't where we find the life God offers. The right path wouldn't land us in pride or burnout. Frankly, if that's what I want, I can chase materialism or higher rank like the unbelievers around me. Superiority and exhaustion seem to be their twin destinations.

But learning and doing can be expressions of something deeper—a relationship.

As we get to know God by embracing the open door He has placed before us, sharing our deepest passions with Him, and listening to Him unfold His nature and purpose to us, learning and doing take on new meaning. I want to know about Him because I am getting to know Him. And the more I know Him, the more clearly I see that life's not about me but about the wonder of His creative and loving expression all around me. The closer I get to Him, the less room there is for pride, because life just simply can't be about me.

> The closer I get to Him, the less room there is for pride, because life just simply can't be about me.

Then the doing makes more sense. Jesus described His own activity as doing what He saw the Father doing (John 5:19). Because of that intimate connection, we too can know God's heart and step into the very moments He has chosen for us.

The Spirit-empowered life certainly has a lot of learning and doing ahead, but no such moments exist apart from the relationship God is growing with us. Jesus promised His disciples that the "Holy Spirit *comes on you*"

(Acts 1:8, emphasis added). On the day that promise was fulfilled, we are told that "all of them were *filled with the Holy Spirit*" (emphasis added), showing God's intent to no longer occupy centralized buildings but to dwell within the hearts of His people (John 14:16–23; 15:1–7; Eph. 2:21–22; 1 Cor. 6:19–20).

That so-called indwelling reveals a relationship of great intimacy and depth, something well beyond the moments of temporary empowerment described in the Old Testament. God engages those who follow Him in a relationship that gives the needed context for every subsequent step of learning and doing. Essentially, because I am in Him and He is in me, I want to know Him more and serve Him with my whole heart.

That's the life He gave to His disciples, and that's the life He has for us. We call it a Spirit-empowered life!

THINK ABOUT IT

1. What does a relationship with God mean to you?
2. Why do you think people substitute learning and doing for knowing God?

CHAPTER 11

Relationship: Does God Truly Want This?

S o what does God want? Clearly that's a question we must grapple with, isn't it? After all, the very idea of God demands that we give some thought as to any agenda or purpose He might have in our world, because if He has one, wouldn't ignoring Him be a bit foolish? You bet it would.

Still, lots of people play hide and seek with a God who really wants to be found.

Why does God want to be found? What does He want? Each of the many religious systems that dot human history offers an answer. Some think God designed us to be slaves to His unpredictable whims. Others assume He has a standard for us to reach toward, and those who fail end up getting "zapped." Still others think we have an assignment to complete and He'll stop by at some point to see if we're getting stuff done.

But let's think that through a bit better.

If God wants us to build Him something, to make something happen, or to construct spectacular buildings for Him, wouldn't it work better if He did that Himself? After all, a quick scan at His handiwork proves He can do much better than we can. If God wanted us to manufacture something for Him, wouldn't it make more sense to give us abilities that more closely match His expertise? I mean, if He wanted people to build Him cool things, He had to sit and wait a long time for us to progress through the Stone Age, the Bronze Age, and a few others before we finally got to the days of iron where we could build stuff that lasts.

If He wants us to meet some standard, master a behavioral template, or get a perfect score on His judge's card, well, that ship has sailed, hasn't it? If God wants us to be what we clearly can't be, isn't it time to start over with a more superior model of . . . well, us? Those who insist that God's goal is to get us to measure up to His level of right choices don't offer a world with much hope.

Many in the ancient world thought their gods created us to carry water for them or help them satisfy their insatiable urges. Those ideas didn't exactly create a life to be thankful for, as the demands had a tendency to shift depending on what the representatives of these gods seemed to want.

What could God want that would actually require our involvement? Keep in mind that God doesn't lack anything. He is completely self-existent, which is a bigger way of saying self-sufficient. He's not lonely, nor does He need us to keep His pantry stocked with animal sacrifices. He's not short on anything and could just as easily exist without us. It's fair to say that while many of us have realized that we need Him, He actually has no need of us.

And we certainly aren't His peers. We can't and don't do anything on His level. Anything and everything we do falls well short of what He can do without us. Want to build a great tower? God can smile and wink a far better

> The Bible makes it clear that God wants us to connect with Him.

one into existence and move it around with His smallest finger. We can't live one day at the level of His goodness, nor do we have much intelligence beyond what one day usually requires.

So what does He want, and what could we possibly bring Him that He can't or won't take from us?

The only possible answer is relationship—a connection He doesn't force on us. The Bible makes it clear that God wants us to connect with Him, but He won't flip us to automatic mode to make that happen. We can only respond to His offer by faith—the choice to believe what He has shown us about His intent.

Now, I can't begin to imagine why God would care to have a relationship with me. I have nothing to offer Him. But somehow He has decided that He wants to make Himself known to me so I can choose to know Him and find the life He gave me to live. That's His plan, and that's His purpose. The choice to respond is the only thing I can bring to Him.

If you're looking for some explanation of your specialness that would justify His interest, well, good luck with that because it's not there. Yet God has chosen to make this relationship matter to Him—matter enough to pay a remarkable price so it could happen.

Several times in the Old Testament, we learn that God wanted to dwell with people. He wanted to hang with Adam and Eve in the pristine garden of Eden (Gen. 3:9), but they chose differently. He wanted to walk the Israelites to their new land of promise, but they asked Him to keep His distance (Ex. 20:19). Then, when they got to the edge of their incredible futures, they picked out pictures in *Better Homes and Deserts* and decided to stay there instead.

He gave them a tabernacle, dwelt in a temple, and even moved into an inferior version while they recovered from another set of idolatrous mistakes. Finally, He told them that the day would come when He would check out of buildings and live in their hearts—a possibility He has kept on the radar for some time now. How does it happen? By our choice to believe Him, follow after Him, and live alongside Him.

Now here's the crazy part: He wants this living with us to last forever!

That's right! Heaven is God's choice to live with us for always. Sure, it's heaven for us because we get a new address inside the perfect city He has designed. It's heaven for us because all the hurtful things that have marred the beauty of His intent will be gone. It's heaven for us because each of the limits of our capacity will be lifted. It's heaven for us because we get to be with God every day!

And somehow, it's heaven for Him because we are with Him for eternity. Honestly, I can't imagine why God would want me for a neighbor, but He has shown me quite clearly that He does.

As we have said, God did all the heavy lifting to allow us to get past the barrier of our own sinfulness. He became the ultimate payment for everything we did without Him. And He has removed every barrier to what He has wanted all along—relationship with you and me. Wow!

> I want to give myself to His mission, because it feels like it's both the most and the least I can do.

So why do we think our perfection is the necessary ticket? He's pretty much settled our failure and picked up the tab. So how will spit-shining our daily weaknesses make us more acceptable to Him? And why would we think He's fingering the cosmic zapper, just waiting to jolt us when we miss the mark? A God who died for our sins isn't likely to be waiting to criticize our next stumble, is He?

Instead, He loves me and offers me new life, and I want to embrace that new path—not so I'll be good enough, but so I can show Him how grateful I am for the life He's offered. And I want to give myself to His mission, because it feels like it's both the most and the least I can do. God wants me to know Him and live with Him and encounter a God-sized journey that He has created for me.

And the mission? Well, as much as God wants relationship with me, that matches how much He wants relationship with every other individual breathing the atmosphere around me. Jesus tells us He doesn't want anyone to miss out on this relationship and spend eternity at a different address (Matt. 18:14).

That's why God shows up in your life and mine. That's why He prompted the prophets of old to tell His story in their generation and to help us see His hand in human history. That's why God reveals Himself in every generation, sometimes in ways that all can see and sometimes in a manner that only those ready to believe can perceive. He makes Himself known because He wants us to know Him and find the unique and remarkable life He has designed for us.

He wants relationship, and He brings His best resources to those who want that, too. That's why Jesus promised an abundant way of living—not to make kings out of us, but because the King of the universe has been knocking on our door.

Why does He want that? I'm not sure I can offer a good answer to that. The why eludes me, but the fact simultaneously amazes me. It's His agenda, His purpose in this majestic creation. The evidence clearly shows that relationship is His passion, and I don't want to miss a minute of that, do you?

Like the great apostle Paul said, "I want to know Christ" (Phil. 3:10–12). Apparently God wants that, too!

THINK ABOUT IT

1. What do you think is the most amazing part about God's grace?
2. Given that God loves you and has opened the door so you can find everything you need for life, how do you want to live?

CHAPTER 12

Relationship: Where It Starts

So this is where it all starts. God's unlimited creativity means that a Spirit-empowered life will end up looking different for each of us. The path you'll find is unique, the purpose specially designed around your set of talents. The ways God will propel you forward will have you telling your own remarkable story someday around a heavenly water cooler. There's really no way to fully imagine everything the road ahead might look like. That makes the discovery even more exciting.

But your starting line will look a lot like mine.

Yes, your road to discovering God's presence and desire to connect has its unique twists and turns. You've likely traveled through places I've not seen, and I have a few stops that never hit your itinerary. While our roads might have little in common, they end up converging into a similar passage. Relationship with God starts in the same place for you, for me, for old-timers, and those yet to be conceived. Jesus made it clear that there's only one way to the Father. We've got to travel through Him (John 14:6).

Chances are reasonable that if you spent money on a book with this title, you've probably taken the first steps to an active relationship with God. After all, most people who want a Spirit-empowered life have some inkling of the Spirit offering the power. Of course, you may have thought this book was about something else, or maybe a friend shoved this book in your hands with some sort of an invitation to do what you're doing now, "Here, read this."

Regardless of whether or not you feel like you've engaged this relationship, I'm convinced this chapter is for you—perhaps to mark out a new path and a life-altering moment or to make the road you've already chosen a bit more clear. Even if you've earned a decade or more of frequent-flyer miles in a padded church pew, you may need to rediscover the relationship you've engaged and what it really means for your life.

A relationship with God grows out of the occasionally awkward merger of want and need. Some have suggested that when God created us, He installed a God-sized hole somewhere near our chest cavity. I'm not sure of the anatomical accuracy of such an idea, but I've heard many people speak of somehow feeling they'd been living with something missing. I recall one young woman saying she felt like she'd been "homesick for a place she'd never been." I think a lot of folks might retweet that.

If you spend any time reading the Jesus stories recorded in the Bible, I know you'll see some interesting stuff. There was something attractive about Jesus. People of all shapes, sizes, and stories wanted to get close enough to touch Him—or more accurately, for Him to touch them. They spoke of His compassion (Matt. 14:14), His extraordinary ideas (7:28–29), and His ability to remove diseases the rest of the people believed to be irreversible (4:24). When Jesus came to town, people came running. They wanted what He had, and after a few minutes, realized that they wanted Him, too.

In my life as a pastor, I've had the amazing privilege of describing God to a lot of different people, and their reactions intrigue me. Some have trouble believing me. They act like they can't believe God could really be like the picture Jesus painted. I smile, recheck my sources, and assure them that God isn't the angry mob waving with protest signs that ridicule their failures. He's not sunning Himself on a distant cloud with little interest in the storms pouring down on them. And He's not stoking hell's fires and giggling at the thought of tossing them in. Yes, He has impossibly high standards, but He lovingly bridged the gap. He offers the same bridge to their purple-haired neighbor, too.

> People like Jesus, and when they get a glimpse of the accurate picture, they usually want what He came to offer.

People like Jesus, and when they get a glimpse of the accurate picture, they usually want what He came to offer.

But there's more than just a "want" that brings you to relationship with God. Somewhere the idea that you need Him begins pressing into your thoughts as well. And until your need reaches a point of action, you have trouble sorting out your want of Him from all the other wants you carry. Need makes you drop the rest of those.

Need grows when your failures move to the center of the stage. Need emerges when you're hungry but can't reach the sweet-smelling cookies on the highest shelf. Need wins when you stand empty-handed because everything you've grabbed for has slipped through your fingers, been taken away, or proven so inadequate that you've tossed it aside willingly. Needing God goes way beyond wanting God and the cool possibilities of the life He offers. Need knows you need what only He can give you.

That's why a relationship with God is often born out of brokenness. Until your need becomes clear, you're not ready to toss your keys to God and move to the passenger seat. If you just want God to drive, you'll usually let Him do that for a bit, then you'll grab the wheel again when something sparkles at the next exit.

Need willingly gives up driving altogether.

So you discover you need forgiveness. You discover you need to break out of some things that feel like binding chains. You discover that you've broken things that keep crumbling with every effort you make to fix them. Need pushes you to discover the dark place a life without God is taking you. Need takes you to the only place where you can start a relationship with God: the end of yourself.

Jesus called it "denying" yourself (Matt. 16:24) and "losing" your life so you can find it (10:39). Honestly, nobody wants that, so need has to meet you at that crossroads before you'll accept its terms. And when you find that place, the conversation usually looks something like this . . .

> *God, I need You. I've failed in so many ways, and I feel so empty inside. I admit it . . . I desperately need You. I've done my own thing long enough, and now I realize that I've been missing what life is really all about. Please forgive me. I know now that Jesus died so I could have life, and that's what I'm desperate for now. Please wash away the stench of my failures and open the door to the life You have for me. I want to believe You have a better way for me to live, and I choose to follow wherever You lead me. I give You my life, and I'm so grateful that You love me and have never given up on me. Now show me where to go and what to do . . . because I'm Yours now.*

That's when relationship starts—an eternity-long connection where each day offers new experiences of who God is and how His amazing plan unfolds before you.

When that relationship starts, the barriers crumble. First, there's the barrier that separated you from God. It comes down the instant you confess your sin and choose to follow God's path. God is absolutely sinless, so you can't walk beside Him and engage this connection until you let Him wash that mess away. But when you do, He does it instantly (1 John 1:9). How amazing is that?

Other barriers begin falling, too. The barrier that kept you from being the person you were designed to be is next. Those chains around your feelings are now broken. God hasn't just given you a clean slate, you now have the power to walk away from even the most crippling addictions (Gal. 5:1). Jesus sets you free, and that means you are free indeed (John 8:36).

Even the barriers you've built between yourself and others have no more strength to stand. God's love now fills your heart, giving you the capacity to share the forgiveness you've been given. We'll journey through that more in the next section, but God starts giving His people the power to conquer those issues and makes healing a lot of past hurts possible.

Now a door has been opened to the world you've been wanting. So step in. There's a life to engage and a journey of purpose and extraordinary Presence ahead of you.

When the life-changing power of God begins to stir within the lives of His people, everything changes. And that miraculous reality is unleashed when we come to God, bringing both our want and our need. That's the life-changing intersection that will ultimately launch us into the Spirit-empowered life, an intersection we will revisit again and again on the road ahead.

Why? Because it's the only way we can approach God, and it's all we bring to the equation. The Spirit will empower us and equip us for an amazing life, but we must come hungry and own the truth of our complete inadequacy. Only God can bring supernatural capacity to our lives and give us the ability to meet its challenge. Only God can propel us beyond the limits of our thinking and our strength. Only God can generate a heart within that will keep us reaching for the furthest edges of His mission field.

I want that life, and everything I need to live it can only be found in Him.

THINK ABOUT IT

1. To what degree have you truly given your life to God?
2. How has your desire to know God grown? Do you think it is growing now? How do you know?

CHAPTER 13

Experience: Expecting an Encounter

If relationship is the beginning, then experience is the powerful step forward in the Spirit-empowered life. And it is in experience that we find the difference between religion and a life-changing relationship.

I am puzzled by the contentment many people appear to have manufactured with Christianity as a religion. They seem to have forced themselves into a satisfaction with a single conversion moment, believing that finding a new path is now largely up to them. The possibilities of life in the Spirit are exchanged for life in the church, where training and guidelines seek to work their empty magic on once-deeply corrupted lives. People expect repentance, following a new guidebook, and asking God to help them make better decisions to be enough. Starting over, with a new heart and a new group of friends . . . well, that's the Christian life.

Others who may have drifted even further from a relational ideal receive their induction into Christianity before they have the capacity to choose it. Theirs is a lifelong membership, initiated by a parent's choice during their earliest childhood. So, for some, their connection to Christ and His church can operate like registration in any community group. Membership is maintained even without participation, but the connection to New Testament life proves to be in name only.

Even among Pentecostals, many who embrace both relationship and experience with a wide-eyed exuberance struggle to engage compelling encounters and eventually ask themselves, "Is this all there is?" Followers of Christ who've grown stagnant in their journeys are numbered among virtually every group.

The culprit? Often it's a life limited to learning and doing.

Now, don't get me wrong. Learning and doing both have important parts to play in the Spirit-empowered life. A journey with Christ presents the disciple with much to learn and many opportunities to demonstrate the life within. But when these two elements become disconnected from relationship and experience, they lose their context, their meaning, and their fun. The result is a rules-based religion of good works that most soon find exhausting and more than a bit disappointing. Still, those who peddle such a life keep the game clock ticking, urging others forward with motivational weapons like guilt and the promise of occasional feelings of great satisfaction.

But it's not working.

Today, many people have abandoned the church, despite an increasing desire for experience that's growing rampant in our culture. People who are desperate for meaning and life-changing impact have given up hope of finding such a life among those who follow Christ. The life—the amazing life—that people have found exhilarating in virtually every generation now looks bland and void of real meaning, even to those who regularly occupy padded pews for an hour or so each weekend. They sit and listen to amazing stories from ancient times and wish they could find a life with such world-altering impact. Then they file out of their stained-glass cocoons or ornately appointed warehouses back to their daily lives; what they just heard seems to have little, if any, connection to reality.

It seems that Christianity has lost its steam . . . again.

Unfortunately, history affirms our inability to maintain Christianity's energy from one generation to the next. Most of today's denominational groups were launched with great intensity and wild pursuit of Jesus' ideal, only to slip into a life of "the motions" after a generation or two. Even those who worship with fervency today see the moribund creeping in from the edges. They resist the path toward apathy, especially with stories that highlight the exploits of the few. But the focus of learning and doing has a shelf life that is ultimately determined by the energy and momentum they can generate for themselves.

Where relationship has diminished, I'm left with just me. Where experience has been set aside, then what I currently possess is now my maximum resource. Little wonder that the journey fades. My portion can't maintain its forward movement, isn't sufficient for my children, and appears to be an out-of-date story to tell the grandkids.

Where did the power go?

In Acts 3, Simon Peter and John were headed to the temple area to pray when they nearly walked past a lame man begging on the steps. For most of us, that would be a time for compassion and perhaps pity, but for two

Spirit-empowered disciples, it became a moment of action. The two called to the man, "Look at us!" (Acts 3:4). It was clear they were expecting something to happen beyond their own limited capacities. And something did!

The big question is why.

What made Peter and John think they had anything to offer to a lame man? They seem quite aware of their lacking funds (3:6), but demonstrated complete confidence that they somehow possessed something better. Why would they think the man could be healed? Experience. Not the kind that says, "We've done this before," but a moment of experience in their own lives that made them feel ready.

Jesus had told them, "You will receive power" (Acts 1:8), and that power had come through their remarkable experience in Acts 2:4. They were now equipped for moments like this, where their natural potential was clearly inadequate. Only the supernatural would do, and it did.

Shouldn't there be something supernatural about walking with God? Can He reach into our everyday moments without making them something, well . . . not so everyday?

It all started with experience.

Experience is what you get from God when want and need merge into the same moment. On the day that the promised power came to these disciples and the others, want and need were bosom buddies. Jesus had told them to wait for God to empower them and, while they were ready and willing to carry His Commission to distant places, in truth, they were just willing. Yes, they wanted the promised power. Yes, they wanted to make eternal impact. Yes, they wanted to be obedient to the One who had changed their worlds. But they weren't ready. They needed the promised power even more than they wanted it.

> Experience is what you get from God when want and need merge into the same moment.

✻ And it came. ✻

We've already seen how the day of Pentecost transformed Simon Peter from a weak Jesus follower melting at the accusations of a servant girl into the bold voice that proclaimed God's salvation to a massive and somewhat suspicious crowd. Now that power exploded through him, not in words, but in the extended hand that pulled the man to his now-strong feet.

That power flowed from the moment where want met need. This time, the disciples' desire to heal, coupled with a physical need that overmatched their own capacities, dissolved into something bigger than the people on that temple step had seen before. And the man went with them into the temple "walking and jumping, and praising God" (Acts 3:8). The promised power was evident. Two fishermen pulled a man from the drowning depths of his own suffering as easily as they might have once scooped fish from their nets.

As you read a story like that, the obvious question changes from, "How'd they do that?" to "Is it possible that I could do that?" Suffering hasn't been eliminated, need is all around us, and most of us really want to do something about it—if we haven't given up on the idea that something can be done.

What we are asking in that moment is whether or not the Spirit-empowered life is still available to those who follow Christ. And the answer is yes! We know it's still available because stories of those who live it still dot the missional landscape, even if such moments haven't come to our neighborhood for quite a while. We know it's still available because Christ's mission remains active, and there seems to be no decline in the enormous need. We know it's still available because the same God who launched their mission invites us to ours.

So what must you do? Hear Jesus' words for yourself as though He looked at you when He spoke them, "You will receive power when the Holy Spirit comes on you . . . " (1:8).

Yes, you've been given much-needed forgiveness and an invite to the relationship of an eternal lifetime. Yes, you've been invited beyond the threshold and into God's remarkable presence as He takes up residence within you. But the focus has now shifted from within you to beyond you, and the mission that beats within His heart is learning to beat within yours.

If you're going to run with that mission, fulfilling purposes and facing challenges that easily overmatch your limited strength, you need something you don't yet possess. You're going to need an experience that propels you to the next step of God's purposes in your life.

You're going to need that power, too, if you're going to live the life you were made for. Your own learning and doing won't get you there, no matter how rightly motivated these might be. Your own abilities will be no match for the moments ahead, though you may wear compassion on your shirt sleeve. Your want and their need may be ready to rise up all around you, but something needs to happen before you're ready to run up those temple steps.

You need an experience . . . a promised experience that lifts you to that place where wishing you could help becomes, "Look at me!"

You need the power of the Holy Spirit.

THINK ABOUT IT

1. What would it have been like to experience the miracle of Acts 3 from Peter and John's point of view?
2. Do you long to experience the kind of power evident in these men's lives? Describe your own hunger for God to bring His promised power to your life.

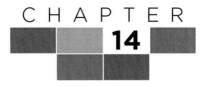

CHAPTER
14

Experience:
Freely Receive

Over the past century, those who believe that New Testament Christianity can be lived in modern times (including the Acts 2:4 power encounter)—the so-called Pentecostals—have been described as people of experience. The moniker isn't usually complimentary, but rather chides their tendency to prioritize the pursuit of emotional moments and unique encounters instead of a more studied approach to life.

Yes, at times the criticism is justified—especially when obvious obedience is eschewed in favor of the sensational, or when those experiences aren't held to the light of a biblical standard. But the emphasis on experience is an absolute necessity and is usually the missing piece in a learning-doing approach to the Christian life. Experience matters a lot.

Since our journey with Christ is driven by want and need—our desire for His purposes and our need for the capacity to fulfill them—experience becomes absolutely essential. We can't give what we don't have or do what we aren't naturally equipped to do. Christians of all theological underpinnings will agree that mankind's nature doesn't naturally go God's way or do godlike things. Those human tendencies are aimed toward self-preservation and self-centeredness. Left to ourselves, the Bible says, we will find the path of destruction (Prov. 16:25).

So how can we engage life at a higher level? How can we join Jeremiah's "run with horses" when we're easily wearied with the race of rats? How can we do what isn't natural for us to do and build life on a path we could never find on our own? Something has to happen. Something must change. And that something is experience.

We can read a good book, challenging us to a better brand of living. The Bible itself offers such counsel. We can also hear great sermons calling us to a new way to live, and we can feel quite sincere in our desire to reach for that life. But can we walk from that moment and simply go do as we're told? Can we just decide to change our stripes and shape ourselves into imitators of Christ? Many church leaders seem to think so. They have great confidence in what knowledge can produce, so those who follow their insights work diligently at the learning and doing paradigm every day. And they do so with occasional, but rarely lasting, success.

But while this "do-it-yourself" approach to following Christ conveys a sense of personal responsibility, it's seldom accompanied by deep satisfaction or supernatural living. Instead, as we've already seen, pride and exhaustion are more likely companions. In such settings, Christianity often will be characterized by its content or its tweetable statements rather than as a relationship that proves life-changing.

Real life-change demands something more, *and that something is experience!*

Something must happen—a moment of empowering or renewed discovery of the power once received. An experience, an encounter with Christ Himself, is what changes our course. Like Saul of Tarsus's pony ride down the Damascus road (Acts 9:1–9) or Jacob's all-night wrestling match (Gen. 32:24–32), these moments are necessary to knock us off our high horses and change the way we walk. We simply can't be talked into a new life direction.

Remember that what Jesus wants us to do is impossible.

We aren't capable of loving our enemies, forgiving those who have wronged us, or walking a supernatural path to take the good news across the known world. (Wait! He wants us to target unknown places, too!) We have severe capacity issues, don't we? None of those challenges or the dozens of others we will face on the way are within our ability to achieve. And "can't" ultimately means "won't" unless something changes—something we most accurately label "experience."

Jesus knew we would need help. That's why He dedicated a lot of His final teaching moments to talk of the Holy Spirit. John recorded much of this teaching in chapters 13–16 of his Gospel, revealing what Jesus promised the Holy Spirit would come and do. He would teach, guide into all truth, convict of sin, and help us remain attached to the presence of Christ (John 14:16, 26). And as we see the early church in action, the presence of the Holy Spirit was absolutely evident.

The apostles did their best to describe these equipping experiences with the Holy Spirit. While a variety of experiences and "gifts" are mentioned, one can't miss the fact that when the Holy Spirit steps into a moment, things become extraordinary. For God to give us what we don't have, it makes sense that He would do it in a manner that we can't. That's the point of the supernatural, isn't it? We know something is beyond us because, well, it comes in a manner that's beyond us.

So a moment of empowering is accompanied by signs and wonders, a need for direction comes with a word of prophecy, an encounter with the sick is met with healing

> One can't miss the fact that when the Holy Spirit steps into a moment, things become extraordinary.

power, and a moment of uncertainty finds an available wisdom, knowledge, or discernment. When want and need merge into a moment, God steps in with the gift we can't find or manufacture.

Spirit-empowered disciples know that everything we need comes from experience, and both the Bible and the Holy Spirit help us understand that experience and how it is intended to alter our current direction. As we have said, this life in the Spirit begins with relationship and grows out of an ongoing relationship with God. It is then fueled and equipped by moments where God gives us what He knows we will need in order to learn and do what He has planned for us.

Everything flows from experience. It has to. We have no other way to be equipped for the impossible path ahead. The apostle Paul promised that God can do far more than we can imagine (Eph. 3:20), but He must make changes in us if we are to participate.

Now isn't that what a relationship with God should be like? Can God walk beside me every day without breaking a few doorframes? Do I really think He intends to live so small in my life that every step will be "me-sized"? Isn't the point of life with God that I can live at a higher level and conquer challenges that are more "God-sized"?

Of course, modern ideas don't often include supernatural expectations. Some corners of the church have rewritten their own understandings of the Bible, making the miracle stories mere misunderstandings of explicable realities. Many Christians try to balance faith in God with a worldview that makes no room for Him. Miracles? He can, but He doesn't, and He probably didn't. So demon-possession is traded for mental illness, leprosy was a misunderstood skin rash, and those dead folk who came back to life were more likely in a coma. No wonder many Christians turn up their noses at the idea of experience. They have explained away the experiences of others, so how would they have faith for some of their own?

I suppose it makes sense that faith would be a part of the experience equation. It's certainly at the core of the relationship we gain with Christ. And when want and need merge in our future moments, we will need faith to believe that God is near and ready to do what we cannot. This is the equation of the Spirit-empowered life.

Of course, want and need don't automatically connect to God. We can shop our lack and hunger in many places. We can turn to numerous alternatives for addressing our weakness. For example, want and need can merge into self-reliance. We can exhaust our own options—and likely ourselves in the process.

We can turn to resources around us and think we've found our answer. After all, if my neighbor has a working lawn mower, I'll borrow his. Why can't I find someone who already has what I think I need and just expect that person to be my necessary source? Never mind that the road in front of me will exhaust that person's resources shortly after my own are gone.

Want and need don't always drive us in the right direction, but when these are found in a heart filled with faith, a path begins to emerge. And that road willingly turns through whatever experiences God makes necessary. When He is the Source, then His is the path, isn't it? The means and the terms are held lovingly in the hands of the One who is our answer.

And He will deliver what we lack through something we call experience. Think about your own life. How has God changed you and what role did an encounter or experience play in that transformation? If you are living a Spirit-empowered life, you know what it means to be deeply affected by the presence of God around you and ultimately in you. If there's no such moment in your memory, your want and need will soon point you in that direction.

Experience matters. There's no life change and no world changing without it.

THINK ABOUT IT

1. When you read the stories of the early church, do you feel adequate to live as they did?
2. In what ways have you experienced God's power?
3. Are you open to whatever experience He may want to bring to your life?

CHAPTER 15

Experience: Power

Tucked somewhere underneath bigger ideas like "heal the sick" and "drive out demons," we find these crucial six words: *"Freely you have received; freely give"* (Matt. 10:8). This small phrase contains the strategy Jesus gave to His disciples as He prepared them for the impossible mission they would one day undertake.

In this particular moment, the disciples were about to experience their first "solo" assignments. Up to this point, Jesus had led every moment. When lepers got close, Jesus stepped forward. When the demonic raged wildly around them, the disciples sidestepped these tormented souls in favor of letting Jesus deal with them. But now, He was sending them out into neighboring villages to tell what they had heard and to do what they had seen done.

In Matthew 10, the disciples received an entire page of instructions—a forty-two-verse instruction manual for ministry that modern Christians seem to overlook. Now, our purpose doesn't give time to consider each point, but again, the real answer to Spirit-empowered living is nestled in the midst of this training session. *I wonder if Thaddeus tweeted it . . .*

Frankly, I can't imagine any of these statements being more necessary than, "Freely you have received; freely give." Because amidst all the cool directives that must have sounded exciting, you know, stuff like "go heal leprosy" and "don't get dusty from rubbing shoulders with those who reject you," and the ominous words about wolves and unfair treatment, the disciples must have been listening for the explanation of *how* they would do such things. You know, "How does this work, Jesus?" I can almost hear Bartholomew ask that, can't you?

That's what I would have asked.

The idea of being in the middle of powerful moments would be exciting and the expectation of resistance might embolden my determination, but if I'm going to be "that guy" in my assigned village, I need to know *how* to be that guy.

Being "that guy" was something the disciples all wondered about. It's why they asked Jesus to teach them to pray—not so they could teach workshops on prayer, but so they could pray like Him and get the kind of results His simple prayers always brought. "What's your secret, Jesus?"

Good question.

The apparent answer came in six words that the Spirit-empowered disciple knows as the only legitimate mantra for ministry life: *Freely you have received; freely give.*

What does that mean? Experience drives everything.

In this initial sending moment, Jesus told His disciples to give what they had been given. He extended His power, authority, and the right to use His name to them for this moment, so they were to give to others what had been given to them. He was saying more than, *I'll be with you doing all the heavy lifting.* Instead, His words clearly implied that He would do in them what He wanted them to do in others.

> His words clearly implied that He would do in them what He wanted them to do in others.

Many Christians live like the four men who carried their lame friend to Jesus. Now these guys provided a great lesson in determination—ripping off a roof so they could lower their buddy closer to Jesus (Mark 2:4). Good job, great faith, and the fifth guy carried his mat home that day.

When I say that many of us live like those guys, I mean that we see our job as bringing people to Jesus so He can heal them, fix their marriages, and solve whatever problems they face.

But when Jesus sent out the Twelve in Matthew 10, and in Acts 1, and in our time and space, bringing people to Him isn't the plan. Instead, He gives us what we need so we can give them what we've got. See the difference? It would have been exhausting for the disciples to carry every lame guy they met either up or down the hill to Jesus.

Now, there's no question that Jesus is the only Healer in their story and in ours, but His plan is to equip us as a conduit of His aid to those in need. He will give us what we need so we can give what is needed to others. And He does that through experience.

Here's a simple example. Have you ever needed to forgive someone?

Honestly, that's not a simple assignment at all, is it? Forgiving is hard work. It requires that you let go of your desire to get even, to set the offender free from the offense, and to pay the price for that forgiveness within yourself. There's nothing in the normal human spirit that either wants to or can truly forgive.

But through experience—the gift of our own forgiveness—Jesus gives us what we need to forgive others. So even though the offended part of our hearts cries, "But, Jesus . . . ," He directs us to remember what we have been given. If God can forgive us of the eternal affronts we've committed against His perfect holiness, don't we need to let go of the offenses others commit against us? We should, we have to, and amazingly, we can.

So the path to giving forgiveness runs through the experience of having been forgiven. In fact, Jesus doesn't just tell us we can forgive others; He says we have to forgive others because of what we've been given (Matt. 6:15).

Are there people who are difficult for you to love? Yeah, me too. But Jesus commands me to love as He loved. In fact, He says that His kind of love is how people will connect me to Him (John 13:35). What does it mean to love like Jesus? Well, it's more than just being willing to die for my friends.

Loving like Jesus has to include both who He loved and how He loved them. While Jesus loves everybody, His mission statement emphasized that He loved those whom no one else was loving (Luke 4:18–19)—and I know that He loved them first, before they had any idea of who He was or what He could do for them. He loved them (and us) even before they had met, and certainly before anything that resembled faith or good deeds began to show up in them.

> Loving like Jesus has to include both who He loved and how He loved them.

Can you love like that? Wow, that goes beyond my original equipment, too. I can love people who love me, and I try to be nice to most everyone else, but loving like Jesus loves seems an impossible hill to climb. And it is, until I realize that I've been given that same unlikely love.

Yes, that's right! I've experienced Jesus' brand of love so somewhere in my life is a reservoir to draw that kind of love from. He gave me that love so I could give it to others—you know, freely received . . .

This is really good news. You see, everywhere that want and need merge in my path, where desire to serve Jesus meets my inability to be that guy on my own, Jesus promises to give me what I need. His Holy Spirit will equip me in those moments, either giving me what I need or bringing to the surface what I've already been given. I don't have to manufacture the ability or find my own way around my self-interest. I bring my desperate need to Him, and He gives me what I need or helps me learn how to use my current equipment so I can channel what I've been given toward someone else's need.

Wow! That's good news! Frankly, the idea of being "Jesus with skin on" (as one friend puts it) seems impossible most days. But Jesus doesn't send us out without equipping us. He gives us what we need with the expectation that we will give what we've been given to others. That's how we know we can forgive, we can love, we can spread hope, and we can extend His life-changing power to others. He promises to pour in, and if we will pour out . . . well, He'll keep pouring in.

So the Spirit-empowered life is driven by these experiences of pouring in and pouring out. God gives to us that we might give to others. The more willing we are to pour out, the more willing He is to pour in.

I'm just the conduit. Now, if you're like me and not much of an electrician, let me explain the little I know. A conduit is the channel through which electrical wiring travels from the source to the need. An electrician spends much of his life pushing cable through a conduit as he spreads the needed power throughout a building. Once the conduit is in place, he can connect the electrical power to a light fixture, a dimmer switch, or the receptacle to plug in the lava lamp you've kept since college. The conduit is how the power gets to where it is needed.

But no one says, "Your house has great conduit!" In fact, the conduit is barely noticed as the real source gets credit for every moment that its power is on display. The conduit does its job when it receives power and spreads that power to the targeted places. No credit needed or deserved, but conduit makes the widespread evidence of that power possible.

That's what Jesus meant when He told His disciples they would do "greater things" than He had done (John 14:12). No, they wouldn't top raising people from the dead nor would they find miracles to perform that Jesus had never tried. It wasn't the quality of "things" that would exceed those Jesus had demonstrated—it was the quantity. Their lives would provide conduit throughout Jerusalem, Judea, Samaria, and even to the most distant spots on the planet. Greater means a single, remarkable light will become a thousand points of light and even more!

This is the means by which Jesus' enormous Commission can be fulfilled. He pours in what we need, and we pour out everywhere we go. What other strategy could allow a few dozen folks, living under the thumb of a dominant empire, to ultimately change the world?

Jesus has called each of us to that same world-changing mission, and He has promised to equip us in the same way He empowered His original team. So what has God already done in your life? What will help you step into the need you'll encounter today? What challenges might tomorrow hold? Don't be afraid. He will give you what you need or help you see that it's already in your backpack. That's the way experiencing God really works. In your past, present, and future, you'll find moments with God to empower you for the amazing life ahead.

All you have to do is freely give.

THINK ABOUT IT

1. How do you feel knowing that God has promised to give you everything you need to do what He will ask you to do?
2. Are you ready to experience God's power? Explain that desire as you talk to God today.

CHAPTER

16

Experience: Learning to Wait

J esus promised, "You will receive power"—power to be witnesses, to fulfill the assignment, to do greater things—*power!* This was no casual promise or generic reference to the occasional work of God around them. Sure, Jesus could have launched His disciples with the guarantee that He would show up in unexpected moments and handle their challenging situations—just like He had been doing.

Instead, He said *they* would receive power, the same power of the Spirit that He claimed as His own source. The Holy Spirit would *come upon* them and His power would be *in* them (Acts 1:8).

When the disciples asked Jesus to teach them to pray, this was their dream. They wanted to understand the clear connection Jesus had with the Father, a connection that allowed Him to do amazing miracles. They wanted to do such things, too, and here Jesus told them that power was coming.

Their final conversation with Jesus, the one Luke records in the first chapter of the book of Acts, isn't the first time Jesus spoke of this gift of the Holy Spirit. Much earlier in their journey, He promised that this gift was available to those who asked (Luke 11:13). And John records Jesus' lengthy teaching about what this gift would mean for their lives (John 14–16). Clearly, the implications of this promise had been the point all along: *You will receive power!*

Now God promises us a great many things, doesn't He? We treasure His promises of hope and eternal life. We relish the moments of healing and other clear interventions into our daily struggles. We're grateful for all He teaches us about life, and it's absolutely amazing that God promises to live alongside us and in us as we walk His path. But the promise most clearly in focus as Jesus prepared to return to God's throne room was this: *You will receive power.*

Given that God was handing His missional purposes to a somewhat odd band of followers, power and capacity were essential. The would-be church stood at the precipice of a worldwide launch, which underscored the need for such a power transfer. Yes, Jesus came to live as God's demonstration and He died to make our forgiveness possible, but He also came to usher in a kingdom—one that would go forward through the power of the Holy Spirit. And that Spirit will fill those who follow Christ, embrace the truth of His deity, and stand ready to proclaim His message. One

> One could argue that this promise of power is the most essential of all God's promises in fulfilling His mission.

could argue that this promise of power is the most essential of all God's promises in fulfilling His mission.

The Holy Spirit will come upon you.

The disciples had been mesmerized by the stories since childhood—Gideon leading a tiny strike force against a superior army with torches and pottery as their primary ammo; Samson ripping the gates of a great city from their colossal hinges and carrying them to the top of a nearby hill; and David fearlessly standing up to a bear, a lion, and a Philistine giant, all with this Spirit upon them. Now, the Son of God had promised that the same power would not only come upon them but would be *in* them (John 14:17). What imaginations could such a promise make reality?

A few days later, that promise became reality. Gathered in a simple room, praying—the only thing they knew to do—things suddenly changed. Luke's effort to describe it had to be limited to metaphor. How does one describe in human vocabulary the immense entry of God's presence into a room? *Rushing wind . . . shaking house . . . descending fire . . . unknown tongues*, the indescribable described, the ecstatic normalized into a sentence. Since he wasn't there himself, I can imagine most of his interviews ending with, "Seriously, Dr. Luke, you just had to be there."

Good people, devout and sincere, uncertain yet willing, anxious yet somehow confident of a promise they couldn't describe, had become the first of a Spirit-empowered generation. More than the presence of God had come to them. His power had been poured into them, seemingly without measure, and all thoughts of future destinations had been rewritten. Life had suddenly catapulted to a new level where an amazing future was not only possible but seemingly assured. Boats would no longer be tools for gathering fish; they would be transports for fishers of men.

Any open-minded reading of the book of Acts must acknowledge its stories as the remarkable movement of the Holy Spirit. Yes, they were the acts of the apostles, but the real story lies deep within them—the spread of kingdom hope and truth driven by the Holy Spirit's power. God's mission had been launched and moved faster and more widely than Dr. Luke's research could possibly manage. John said that a written record of everything Jesus did would fill a worldwide library (John 21:25), the full works of His Spirit-filled army would likely have demanded an even larger number of shelves. God had poured and continued to pour His Spirit into those early believers with world-changing results. Spirit-empowered people don't find their historical hope in Acts 2 alone. Chapters 4, 9, 10, and 19 offer shouts of affirmation as well. Repeatedly, God responded to their wants and needs with moments the translators labeled "outpourings." This gift wasn't just for the 120 people in the upper room; God kept pouring until the apostles realized this was His plan for all who would take up His cause. Those who once persecuted Christians weren't eliminated. Gentiles didn't have to wait outside the door. Distant peoples in distant places could claim this promise and encounter its life-changing force no matter where they might have been and what they might have been doing on the day of original outpouring. The extraordinary became the normal expectation of God's people.

> The extraordinary became the normal expectation of God's people.

You will receive power means *you!*

In Acts 19:2, Paul encountered a group of Christ-followers and immediately asked them a most pressing question, "Did you receive the Holy Spirit when you believed?" You don't need to be a theologian to see Paul's clear understanding that something more was available to those who believed. These believers had received John's baptism after their decision to repent of sin and receive the kingdom of God brought by Jesus. Some think these guys had heard of John but not Jesus—that this was their moment of salvation. But Paul didn't ask about their connection to Jesus. Instead, his question centered on whether or not they had received the power of the Holy Spirit. They had believed the testimony of John, they had demonstrated faith in John's cousin Jesus, but they had not received the Holy Spirit's power. They had not been launched into the powerful destiny God intends for His witnesses. Like the disciples in Acts 1, there was something more for them to receive, and they did.

So let's imagine Paul's question echoing through the centuries until it now rings in our ears. "Did you receive the Holy Spirit when you believed?" Have we been launched into the Spirit-empowered life through the fulfillment of Jesus' promised gift?

Some have decided that the gift and the unique moments that accompany it were just for those early guys, you know, to get things started. But the evidence says otherwise. In fact, the same prophetic passage Peter quoted in his Acts 2 sermon—recorded in Joel 2—says that God's intent is to pour His Spirit "on all people" (Joel 2:28). There's no indication that He meant a single calendar date. He specified the impact on sons and daughters, too, proving that no gender and generations were excluded.

This promise is for us, just waiting for our want and need to bring us to the place of receiving. Those who desire to take up Jesus' mission, to give their best to His worldwide agenda, and raise their hands to His purposeful cry quickly realize their own limited capacity. Want meets clear need, for who can do the work of God besides God alone? Promised power isn't just an intriguing fantasy, like the idea of the sorcerer who offered Peter money so he could do such things (Acts 8:18–19). No, this genuine desire to impact our world for God must also come with a clear sense of our need. We must have His power, we must have what Jesus said the Holy Spirit would bring. We cannot go into all the world—we can't even go across the street—without the power of God's Holy Spirit within us.

My heart is just as hungry as the centurion's in Acts 10, and my need is just as acute as those guys in Acts 19. I want to give myself to God's eternal purposes, both as life's most meaningful mission and as my best "thank-you" for His gift of salvation. I want to give Him my life, but He must give me His power so I can engage the life He intends. I need the Holy Spirit to come upon me.

And He will. And Jesus said to wait until He does (Acts 1:4–5).

So how will you know when He has come?

Believe me, you'll know.

Of all the uncertainties we see in the lives of the early disciples, this was something they were sure of. They had been filled with the Holy Spirit. Their moment had been flooded with the overwhelming presence of God. Their room had come alive with His awesome presence. They didn't enter such moments knowing what would happen, but stuff happened. God doesn't bring His power into a room without folks knowing it. No mystical secrets here, no quiet outpourings while others in the room casually eat their lunch. Their moment had disrupted all activity. God had come in power, not in the gentle whisper Elijah once heard.

As these early believers described their experiences during Dr. Luke's interviews, their level of detail varied a bit, but one common thread was the receipt of a new language. Praises to God they had formed in their minds took on the new syllables of different languages, some human and some perhaps heavenly, but all unknown to the one now shouting them. The Holy Spirit had come and apparently enlisted the disciples in a choir that sang from an unknown hymn book. This speaking in tongues had been a part of the great day of Pentecost (Acts 2:4), and later proved to Peter that the same Spirit had come to the Gentiles (10:44–46). They were a part of the story again in Acts 19, as those disciples could now say yes to Paul's question, and we can expect that they'll be a part of our empowering moments as well. God doesn't pour out His power with a whimper. He lights up the room and leaves no doubt that everything has changed. None of these first-century friends knew exactly what would happen, but things certainly did. And when the glorious moment had subsided, they knew things would be different forever.

Some folks react negatively to the idea of speaking in unknown tongues or engaging additional experiences they might find in their own upper rooms. Their comfort zone prefers to encounter God on their terms, within their own prescribed boundaries. But doesn't it make sense that receiving a power greater than you has to push you beyond, well . . . *you?* Tragically, many never allow their hunger for God's power to grow so unbounded. They choose borders for their relationship with the eternal One, unknowingly creating too small a box to receive His full plan for their lives.

Real hunger throws off such restrictions. Real hunger longs for the presence and power of the Holy Spirit in as full a measure as God will bring. Real hunger sees the One experienced rather than stumbling over preferences regarding the things that come in His wake.

Talk to people who have been there. Ask them to describe their initial moment of empowering and see if they can tell the story without tears filling their eyes. Most will have far more to say about what God was doing in them at that moment than what they were doing in response. That's what hunger for God's Spirit looks like.

So Paul asks again, "Did you receive the Holy Spirit when you believed?"

If not, let God hear about your hunger. Let Him see how much you want what He wants, and convince Him that you know how much you need His help to do what He has asked of you. Bring your want and need to Him, and He'll show you that His promise is for you, too.

You will receive power . . .

THINK ABOUT IT

1. Think about Paul's question in Acts 19, "Did you receive the Holy Spirit when you believed?" How do you answer that?
2. If you haven't received the Holy Spirit, are you hungry for the power God has promised? Are you ready to receive it? Begin thanking God for that promise, and tell Him of your desire to receive so you can be a powerful part of His missional plans.

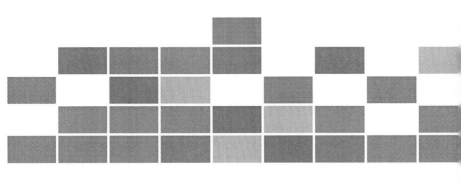

THE
DEMONSTRATION

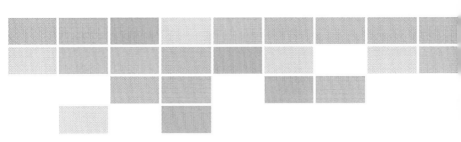

CHAPTER 17

Connect: The Priority Is People

Those who engage the Spirit-empowered life quickly discover something unusual about relationship with God: Life is people-focused. There can be no isolation, no separation where it's just God and you, because God has a greater purpose to share. And that purpose is connecting with others.

I once met a man who insisted he had no need for other people. He expressed great contentment in the idea that He and God could exist together quite happily in his farmhouse and barn. People seemed to get in the way of his efforts to be the man he wanted to be. So he treated most of us somewhat belligerently and was usually anxious to get back to his own space where it was just him and God—and, of course, the wife he seldom nurtured. In fact, the man told me that his wife would probably be coming to my church, but I wouldn't be seeing him much. He didn't need that sort of thing.

He's not far from an idea others have held throughout the centuries: A relationship with God is most easily lived in separate spaces, away from temptation, distraction, and a lot of other stuff they would prefer to blame on others. So whether they formalize such an approach in a monastery or functionally try to keep everyone out of their business, the belief is that their relationship with Christ is just that—theirs.

> His plan, and the subsequent way He wants to connect each of us to it, involves people.

It's just that . . . well, a relationship with God is a connection with One who is coming toward people. Yes, there are special moments when He speaks tenderly to us in an individualized way. Yes, He addresses the uniqueness

100

of each individual's journey and places His finger on the elements of each personal life that need some work. Yes, God has a specialized plan for my life and a completely different one for you, but there is no isolation. His plan, and the subsequent way He wants to connect each of us to it, involves people.

We've already considered the amazing idea that God wants to be with us. No, we're not deserving, and yes, it's puzzling to figure how a perfect God could find pleasure in time spent with imperfect us. But His clear plan, revealed throughout human history and in the person of Jesus, is to be "God with us."

And that also means, *God with them.*

When Jesus intruded into the lives of a few young fishermen, it was with the promise that they would someday fish for men. I wonder if they wanted to. Like most of us, they probably were a bit more focused on hanging out with a possible Messiah candidate. They were likely imagining that a chance to be a part of His kingdom meant being in charge of people, getting their own ways for once, and rising above their mediocre existence. When we look at how they struggled to embrace some of Jesus' teachings, it doesn't seem like they were thinking about a chance to serve people, does it?

But that's who God is. This connection is with One who wants to have a lot of other friends, too. And the mission He's invited us to undertake is all about helping other people find what we've found. There's no exclusivity here.

I'm not sure we get that vibe in the local church.

Sadly, some churches seem to prioritize isolation. Their mostly empty buildings and half-vacant pews seem to lack room for anyone else. Rare is the thought of reaching out to others. If you want to find your way into such churches . . . you can. But they're doing what they do and don't have time for distractions like you. These kinds of churches are dying, and it's difficult to decide whether or not that's a bad thing.

Spirit-empowered disciples function with a completely different mentality. We know God has launched us into the people business, and we look for every opportunity to demonstrate that a relationship with God is possible. We see others as Jesus saw them—like sheep with no shepherd (Matt. 9:36)—and we know that the Shepherd we have found has room in His flock.

Now, there are many reasons why God has given us His Holy Spirit, but chief among them is to empower us to be His witnesses (Acts 1:8). Already, we have repeatedly reflected on the message and implications of this verse. By saying that His followers would be witnesses in Jerusalem, Judea, Samaria, and to the ends of the earth, Jesus revealed that His clear intent was to send His guys to Jerusalem, Judea, Samaria, and to the ends of the earth. These words weren't meant to be fodder for missions' theory. People, near and far, need to hear what we've heard and see what we've seen. So "go" isn't figurative. He gives us His power so we can do what He has called us to do.

This unique kingdom isn't just about us.

Yes, God has a lot planned for us and a lot of good things to give to us, but we only receive by giving. In one of His oddest statements, Jesus said that we would find our lives when we lose them (Matt. 10:39). He introduced several unusual ideas in His teachings, truths that go against the grain of the expected, and sometimes preferred, ideas of our culture.

He said His kingdom was about "Him and them." When asked which of God's many commandments was most important, Jesus had a somewhat surprising answer. Shouldn't He have said, *All of them! If God said it, then that makes it really important, so be sure and make every single command your priority.* But He didn't equivocate like that. Instead, He answered, seemingly without hesitation, "Love the Lord your God with all your heart and with all your soul and with all your mind" and "love your neighbor as yourself" (Matt. 22:36–39). He went on to say that all the commands connect with these, but the real point is He answered the question.

That answer shows us the priority of His kingdom—*Him and them.*

In another place, Jesus told us to "seek first his kingdom and his righteousness," and then everything we worry about will be cared for in our lives (Matt. 6:33). In other words, when we focus on Him and them, God will take care of us.

There's that unusual idea. If we live as if life is all about us, we lose. But if we live to worship Him and love them, He will take care of us! Pretty remarkable strategy, isn't it?

This is what Spirit-empowered people understand. We live with a sense of calling—a purpose greater than any selfish agenda. We know that loving God and loving others are the only ways to fulfill the Great Commission. It's only as we obey these two commands that we find ourselves connected to the One we claim to follow (John 13:35).

> We live with a sense of calling—a purpose greater than any selfish agenda.

Jesus said that His mission was "to seek and to save the lost" (Luke 19:10).

He described Himself as a good Shepherd—the kind who would leave a pen full of sheep to find one lost lamb (Luke 15:4). He even said that He would lay down His life for His sheep (John 10:11). If we're in a relationship with Him, well, this is the God we are connected to. So thinking this life is about us can't really work, can it?

The Spirit-empowered life is expressed in many different ways, but at its core is the pursuit of people. Jesus desperately sought to get this point across to His disciples, and it proved to be a lesson they struggled to receive.

In one story, Jesus was resting by a well near the Samaritan town of Sychar while His disciples went into the village to get lunch. John tells the whole story, though he only lived the lunch errand (John 4). While he and the other disciples were in town, Jesus and a not-so-righteous woman had a conversation that proved life-changing for her. He uncovered her life's shame and revealed His great compassion, ultimately sending her away with living water that had already begun to quench her deepest thirst.

As she ran back to the village to tell her friends about this man by the well, the disciples returned with food. The text says that they saw Jesus speaking with the woman, but "no one asked" what she wanted (v. 27).

Really? Jesus was speaking to a Samaritan woman, one with a questionable past, and no one asked about it? The conversation set social convention on its ear and no one cared? Apparently John had to get the full story later because he missed his chance for a firsthand interview. *C'mon guys, what are you thinking about?*

Lunch.

Instead of, "Hey Jesus, tell us what just happened," they said, "Rabbi, eat something" (v. 31). And Jesus turned them down. He was not disappointed in their lunch choice or frustrated that there was no ketchup for the fries. His mind was somewhere else, somewhere He wished their minds could find.

"I have food to eat that you know nothing about" (v. 32).

Wow! Surely they were going to catch the meaning behind that cryptic statement. But they didn't. Instead they wondered if someone else had brought Him some food.

So He pushed on, explaining that His food was "to do the will of him who sent me and to finish his work" (v. 34). He went on to beg them to lift their eyes off of the bread in their hands and onto a harvest that was desperate to be picked. "Don't you have a saying, 'It's still four months until harvest'? I tell you, open your eyes and look at the fields! They are ripe for harvest" (vv. 35–36).

Suddenly lunch didn't taste so good.

There's more to life than food. There's something that matters more than our daily stuff. There's a mission with people and amazing stories of life-change to be written. There are damaged women at wells and broken men at bus stops. There are hurting people next door and desperate ones around the world. There's a harvest out there, and more of it is ready for picking than we think.

If we lift up our eyes, we'll see what Jesus sees . . . and only then will we begin to realize what He wants us to do about it.

THINK ABOUT IT

1. Why can't people fulfill God's purposes without a passion for others?
2. What do you think Jesus was trying to get His disciples to see in the story recorded in John 4?

CHAPTER

18

Connect: Redeeming Love

Throughout its nearly two-thousand-year history, the church has had a relationship with its world that can best be described as awkward. In many generations, the relationship has been antagonistic due to the aggressive effort of governments to hinder and even destroy those who follow Christ. Like those in the early church, many of Jesus' disciples have spread His truth under a cloak of suspicion and even outright persecution.

Of course, there have also been eras when governments fully tolerated and even embraced the church and its people. In such cases, Christianity was viewed as the religion of the empire, and its citizens labeled Christians, regardless of the ethics they chose to obey. In these settings, the church was a distrusting partner of monarchs, often wrestling for power by standing on its high moral ground as God's apparent voice to even its king. In such cases, the flipside found that the government often overwrote certain elements of truth while trying to use the religion for political purposes.

In the Western world today, we see both extremes at work. Certainly the church's ideology is under attack and biblical principles are quickly losing their once-influential place in the modern discussion. At the same time, segments of the church have sought to flex political muscle and speak to troubling issues by a variety of means—some Christlike and others seemingly not.

When Jesus said we are in the world but "not of the world" (John 17:14) and Paul challenged us to remember that "our citizenship is in heaven" (Phil. 3:20), they sought an approach to life that believers have always found difficult to demonstrate. Some withdrew to monasteries, while others tried to live so close to the relevant edge they were in constant danger of falling into the worldly chasm.

The church in its world has never been an easy proposition. But when disciples look clearly at Jesus and interpret His mission as our own, the picture becomes clearer. Jesus cared deeply for righteousness but didn't reach for any political methods to achieve it. The dusty streets He walked weren't places of democracy, and the opportunity to influence governmental behaviors wasn't in the scope of influence for a Jew in the Roman empire, but what Jesus could do was love people . . . and He did. In fact, it seems He did that more than anything else.

> Jesus cared deeply for righteousness but didn't reach for any political methods to achieve it.

Nobody was beyond the gaze of His loving eyes. Drunkards, turncoat tax collectors, even prostitutes—their faces so worn by their harsh life they seemed decades older than their ages—these were all intentional targets of life-changing love. The untouchables—lepers who wore their disease on the surface and religious folk who tucked theirs inside—could be touched and changed if they would come close.

God is love (1 John 4:8).

Young John watched that truth up close and never got it out of his mind. As an old man, he still marveled at the love he had seen all day long in Jesus' warm eyes and tender hands. There was simply no one Jesus wouldn't walk toward. Even half-naked lunatics—driven away until cemeteries became more than their symbolic homes—came running, with demons stopping dead in their tracks.

If the same Spirit fills us, shouldn't the list of those we embrace look similar?

Too often, Christians who celebrate having been lifted from sin's depths forget where they came from. After a few years of somewhat cleaner living, they begin to view those still stuck in the mud as inferior, deserving of their soiled futures, and unworthy of their time. In truth, these modern Pharisees now take credit for what only God could have done in their lives.

Those of us who live Spirit-empowered lives hold the image of our former selves in view, and we see our earlier destinies in the broken around us. We remember that the gospel came to us as "good news," and we remain confident that the news is still good for those trapped in their self-styled darkness.

Picket signs seldom proclaim hope.

I've always been troubled by one clear difference between Jesus and us. (Okay, there's a bunch of those, but one bothers me more than the others.)

Why is it that those who seemed furthest from God—the folks who lived the most wicked habits and choices we can label—were generally running toward Jesus, while those who lived righteously, at least on the surface, were among the ones who wanted Him dead?

And why is it, usually, just the opposite for us?

Those trapped in sinful lives drive right by our mega-warehouse churches and tiny chapels with little interest in what might be available inside. Most of our neighbors don't even know they weren't at church last Sunday because they never think about it and haven't yet had a reason to think about where we go on Sunday mornings. At the same time, self-righteous people can sit comfortably in our pews and ply their egotistical trade among us with little threat of rebuttal.

Spirit-empowered people see the world like Jesus did.

Jesus was perhaps best known for His eyes of compassion. He couldn't see brokenness without thinking how this wasn't supposed to be. He viewed the sinner as a victim of Satan's slap at His Father. The deceiver had lured the prized creation into his own rebellion, and now God had come with tender eyes and outstretched hand, hoping each would trust Him and believe there was a better way.

That's how we who are Spirit-empowered are learning to see those around us. The work of God's Spirit within us yields love as its primary fruit. How? Once again, it's the merger of relationship and experience. We are overwhelmed with how Jesus wriggled us free from the chains of our own history, and we know His capacity to do the same for others. We see people through the lenses of what we once were and

> We see people through the lenses of what we once were and where we might currently be if not for the undeserved rescue He brought.

where we might currently be if not for the undeserved rescue He brought. There's hope for others because there was hope for us.

No wonder the outcasts came running.

We did too, right? Like John, we discovered that God is, indeed, love. And love changes people. In fact, it's the only thing that ever has.

The book of Romans offers a lengthy proof that law can't redeem—not even God's law. The rules show us our failure and magnify it more power-fully than any microscope or telescope ever could. But it doesn't fix us. So, "what the law was powerless to do . . . God did by sending his own Son . . . " (Rom. 8:3).

That's why Spirit-empowered disciples don't turn up their noses at sinners. There's no surprise when those trapped in Satan's grasp choose to sin. Certain sins may seem shocking, but they are never surprising. What does surprise is that God doesn't run away, and neither do we who have been sent by Him.

Who can't be rescued? Is there anyone who has run so far down the wrong path they can't be retrieved by grace? The stories unfolding around Jesus would seem to shout a resounding no!

Zacchaeus was a notorious cheat, hated by his countrymen for his com-plicity in Rome's thievery, stealing everything they had of value under the guise of taxation. Childhood friends now spat at the mention of his name, and their hatred only grew as he enlarged his house at their expense. He was a small man with an even smaller heart. *And then . . .*

His curiosity to see the peasant teacher drove the proud man to a tree branch, but even he had to be stunned when Jesus stopped and called him from his unique perch. Hours later, after Jesus had disappeared into the tax collector's home, the little man emerged with a new heart and began cashing in his estate so he could bless those he had once cheated (Luke 19:8). I'll bet the local folks never saw that coming!

But if that was a bit of a surprise, the day a group of lepers came back into town with skin pink and whole had to be a shock. Lepers never came home. Their contagious disease marked them as cursed by God, and those who once loved them now considered them dead. But nobody was really dead when Jesus came into the picture. Ten lepers received back ten lives, and ten families now held an impossible gift (Luke 17:11–14). Pretty cool, huh?

John says we could fill the rest of this book and hundreds more if we told every story (John 21:25).

Spirit-empowered people live in this expectation. We don't turn away from the wicked, the needy, the broken, or even those who hide their dark-ness under wealthy wallets and magnificent castles. We run toward such people, knowing that the same redemptive seed that's daily transforming our lives can be planted into any receptive heart and an amazing harvest can begin to grow. Jesus' redemptive work lives on in every generation.

So it doesn't matter if the current government is a friend or foe. As Jesus told a confused Roman governor, "My kingdom is not of this world . . . "

(John 18:36). Someday the entire world will be consumed in His kingdom and no other will remain. Spirit-empowered disciples believe everyone we meet can be invited into that kingdom.

Indeed, Jesus has already invited them, but only our love delivers the invitation.

THINK ABOUT IT

1. Why do you think it's so difficult for us to love the way we've been loved?

2. What must God do in order to help you become a messenger of His redeeming love?

CHAPTER 19

Connect: Who He Loves

The truth is, love is what got Jesus killed. We understand that He came to earth to die, but some were gladly complicit in His death, determined to put an end to Him and His teaching. These were motivated by a few key factors. Yes, He claimed to be God, and in their religious system, one just didn't do that. But as we read the story, it seems Jesus handed them this apparent blasphemy as the excuse they needed to do what they had already planned to do.

The deeper reason they wanted to be rid of Him was His popularity with the people. Jesus loved people they didn't value and gave this "riff-raff" the idea that God was ready to embrace them. They decided they owed it to God to protect His reputation. After all, how could any idea of God's holiness be maintained if these people thought they could get in the door? Of course, they had some interest in protecting their own reputations, too. They didn't need this kind of competition as arbitrators of spiritual leadership. Jesus' idea of God wasn't acceptable and couldn't possibly maintain the superior status they'd worked so hard to establish.

So they resisted Him; and Jesus did very little to pacify their concerns. In fact, He spent His quality time with those other people and seemed barely interested in debating the issues with the religious leaders. Ultimately, He claimed to be from God and even to *be* God, so what to do with Him became an easier question, and the possible answers got nastier.

How does it make you feel to know that God loves people you don't like? Sure, on some level, we know He does because He's God and He's got a really big heart. But if given a choice, surely He'd prefer to hang out with people like us. Except that He doesn't. He seems quite happy if *they* fill the available slots on His social calendar.

Now, don't get me wrong. God loves you, too. It's just that He really loves them . . . and He sees you as one of them.

On one Sabbath morning, in the early days of His ministry, Jesus joined the synagogue worship in His hometown and took His family's turn at reading the Scriptures. Apparently God's pre-planning was amazingly on target because they handed Him the scroll that would convey His true sense of mission. The day's reading brought the words of Isaiah into that worship setting:

> *The Spirit of the Lord is on me, because he has anointed me to proclaim good news to the poor . . . " (Luke 4:18)*

This was His mission statement—the reason He had donned sandals and traversed dusty streets. He punctuated that Sabbath morning with, "Today this scripture is fulfilled in your hearing" (v. 21). In other words, Isaiah's prophecy was no longer futuristic. "The Me is *Me*!"

That made the room buzz for sure. But the importance of what He said was dwarfed by the actual content of what He said. Jesus identified God's target audience in this eternal mission—the poor, the outcast, the oppressed. Boy, they were lucky, weren't they?

You see, many Christians see these words as a special message for the underdogs. Those who sip iced tea while reclining in middle-class lawn chairs tend to think Jesus' good news must sound especially good in the ears of the downtrodden. Yes, He loves us all—even those guys.

But Jesus didn't come to upend the economic hierarchy or empty out human prisons. You see, from God's line of sight, all of us fit into these target audiences. Compared to His original ideal—the one we forfeited with our sin—we are all poor, in bondage, and currently being beaten up by our sin and the Enemy who keeps us held in it.

Jesus wasn't pitting the street folk against the religious leaders. His kingdom doors swung wide open for both. It's just that the latter group didn't see themselves the way God does. They didn't need a doctor because they were pretending not to be sick (Matt. 9:12).

> Spirit-empowered disciples know that our behavioral standards don't make us any more or less worthy of God's love, so we have little difficulty going among the vastly different to proclaim good news.

But we all need Him. There are no imaginary lines between us and those we think are different. Spirit-empowered disciples know that our behavioral standards don't make us any more or less worthy of God's love, so we have little difficulty going among the vastly different to proclaim good news. That's why we often find these people in unexpected places. We open our arms to strangers and to the strange. We are recipients of Jesus' mission and gladly give ourselves to living a bit of Luke 4 in our own lives.

When Jesus announced His promise of power, it was in the context of four symbolic destinations. Jerusalem, Judea, Samaria, and even the ends of the earth are places, real spots you can find on a map, but they can also represent the worlds that surround each of us. Jerusalem was home for the early disciples, that place where family and friends were always nearby. Judea was the countryside, beyond the city walls, the ever-present "out there" that formed a typical boundary to people who traveled on foot. Samaria was as much an idea as a place. For them, Samaria was the undesired, those viewed as lesser, the place no Jew ever put into his vacation planner. Samaria was the ultimate, "Please, God, not there." And the "ends of the earth"? Well, who knows what that could mean? Most hadn't gotten past the first three regions. The ends of the earth meant those places beyond the world they knew. How might they get there? What would they find there? Jesus could have suggested the moon, and they would have had just as easy a time picturing what that would be like.

This is both where and to whom they were headed. He could just have easily said, "everywhere," but these labels brought a much more powerful realization. No barriers, no lines in the sand, no limits as to where or to whom they would go.

And that's where we, the Spirit-empowered, find ourselves.

In the earliest days of the modern Pentecostal movement, a rediscovery of the Spirit-empowered life that began around 1900, the renewed outpouring of God's Spirit sparked a desperate surge toward world missions. Some assumed the unknown tongues of their experience were the languages they would need across the globe. Others made no such assumption but were no less determined to embrace vastly distant places. In fact, one group to emerge from those days—the Assemblies of God—has become one of the largest groups in the world in its first one hundred years. They connect the promise of Acts 1:8 with their own Acts 2:4 experiences and . . . *Spirit-empowered people go!*

Spirit-empowered people also cross barriers. We find "Samaria" both around us and in distant places. Spirit-empowered people shake off natural boundaries of race, ethnicity, economics, and all others to take the good news to those we know are included in Jesus' Luke 4 identification.

We stretch the boundaries of our Judea as well. In Acts 8:4, we're told that those early disciples evangelized wherever they went. "Preached the word" could actually be translated "good newsing," and it underscores a missional life among whomever today's journey might encounter.

Of course, there's no neglecting Jerusalem, either. The friend, the family, the familiar must hear of God's love and be invited to embrace the hope that we've found. Spirit-empowered people connect with anyone and everyone, because we see ourselves as Jesus' targets as well.

Yes, Jesus died loving outcasts. The Spirit-empowered life often comes with that kind of sacrifice. How else can one explain Christian churches in Tibetan mountains and Ecuadorian jungles? One may find terrorist cells in Middle-Eastern cities, but he's likely also to find gatherings of Christ-followers worshipping across the street. Why? Because Jesus came for every individual, and those who share His mission also share His remarkably diverse travel itinerary.

To be Spirit-empowered is to love those who are different from us. How can we do that? Once again, I reflect on my own unlikely relationship with God, and I know that He wants something similar for every tribe and tongue.

So I bring my want and need, my desire to be a part of His plan, and my need for His help and strength, and He empowers me by His Spirit, just the way He promised He would.

> To be Spirit-empowered is to love those who are different from us.

When the apostle Paul and his mentor-friend Barnabas felt compelled to take the gospel to distant places, they gathered with their church friends at Antioch and shared both their want and their need. They knew God was challenging them beyond the familiar, but they couldn't have known the importance of what lay ahead. They had no thought to be catalysts for the worldwide spread of the gospel but knew there was a boat out there with their names on it.

So they shared their passion with friends, and the Christians at Antioch placed their hands on them and prayed. Now we're not given many details about that moment, but the two men departed from that experience having been "sent" in missionary power (Acts 13:3). Relationship and experience launched these apostles into a vast and diverse mission field.

Yes, Jesus loves everyone, but the specific character of His love is that He loves *them*. One could say that He loves those whom no one else currently loves. And that's where the Spirit-empowered are often found—whether on a boat headed toward Cyprus or on a neighborhood street nearby.

It's the incarnation in its rawest form—God coming to us, hope proclaimed to captives by those who share their hardship. To love like Jesus means we love those others keep on the sidelines. We embrace those more easily kept at a distance.

Most anyone can love those who are like them. But Jesus showed us how to love those beyond natural limits by loving those who were significantly inferior to Himself—yes, that's us. And that's what the love of God really looks like. It's a love that demands more than normal human capacity. Such love requires His Spirit, and it may be the clearest evidence that life in that Spirit has been found.

THINK ABOUT IT

1. Who are the people you find most difficult to love?
2. When you think of your community and your daily life, who are the "unlovely" people you encounter? How might you begin to show them Jesus' love by loving them yourself?

CHAPTER 20

Connect: How He Loves

They didn't know who He was. I mean, who expects God to walk into their neighborhood and wave at them from their fishing boat? No one expects God to wait in line at their tax booth. God just doesn't come to places like this. Creators don't sneak into their handiwork through a stable door. And they sure don't do it in one of the poorest cities on the planet.

No, God doesn't go there . . . and no one expected Him to.

When a carpenter's son began accumulating followers, most figured there wasn't much to see. Sure, a crazy prophet had pointed a bony finger his direction, but the guy was his cousin. It seemed more like a ruse plotted over a family dinner—not the entrance of the rightful King of the universe.

So nobody came to Jesus thinking He was the Son of God . . . nobody.

It took years for those who trailed Him every day to begin to grasp His teaching. His miracles did grab headlines, and many turned out to catch a glimpse as He passed by, perhaps to see someone healed, maybe to hear the whispers of what it might mean. But if seeing is believing, most didn't. In fact, it was only after His reappearance, days after a gruesome death, that those closest to Him finally put the pieces together. He was the Son of God—a Roman soldier was among the first to figure it out (Matt. 27:54).

Yet, in spite of their lacking faith, in spite of their unending need for signs, in spite of their continued pettiness in the presence of the God they worshipped elsewhere, He loved them. In fact, He loved them enough to die . . . for them.

When we read the Gospel stories, we seldom grasp the uncertainty that dominated every one of those days. Jesus' question, "Who do people say the Son of Man is?" (Matt. 16:13), likely had more possible answers than the ones that made it into the text. Even the guys with front row seats didn't know. The right answer came out of Peter's mouth, but Jesus quickly pointed out that His impetuous friend didn't think of that on His own. Indeed, the fisherman seemed to forget what he had said a few hours later.

They didn't know . . . and yet He loved them. Think about what that means.

God loves first.

Okay, we all know that, right? But have you seriously thought about what that means? For God to love first means He loves us before we have any idea of who He is. Paul saw it when he wrote, "While we were still sinners, Christ died for us" (Rom. 5:8). That means Christ loved us before we had faith, before we had hope, and while we were still a huge mess!

> For God to love first means He loves us before we have any idea of who He is.

Good thing He did, too, because we'd never have found Him if He hadn't made that first move. He loved us.

That's why Jesus can extend a hand to a woman caught in the act of adultery (John 8:1–11) and pat the head of one washing His feet with her hair (Luke 7:36–50). That's why He could meet the demon-possessed without focusing on how they might have opened those doors. How He could shed a compassionate tear for a woman who was angry at God because her only son had died (Luke 7:11–12).

Yes, it's a miracle that God would love us at all, but it's even more extraordinary that He would love us first. I could see Him insisting that we demonstrate something toward Him first. I could understand if there were some gauntlet a few might find to earn the love He offers. I mean, if we could be good enough or even just a little better, maybe He would show up and offer mercy. Sure, we could master some survival-of-the-fittest game to earn a chance to kneel before Him. That would make more sense—and one compelling television show.

But there's no contest, no previous requirements, no fine print. God loves us first, even when we didn't know He was there. He has life to offer, and yes, He has a better game plan than the ones we've drawn up, but the point is that He hasn't withheld His love until . . . well, until we do anything. Instead, He loves us first!

That's not how I learned to love, and I went to church a lot.

Okay, I grew up in a really good church that did a great job of loving people, but somehow I still emerged with the idea that the church needed me to believe what they believed and become what they'd become before they could make my spot in the family official. You know, think what I think and do what I do, and then we can be friends. That's the way it works, right?

Not with Jesus. If He waited on right thinking and behaving . . . well, He would have been eating the Last Supper by Himself.

Instead, Jesus took the radical step of loving people before they figured out who He was and long before they let His teaching change their behavior. In fact, He loved them knowing it was the only way they'd ever get to that believing step or trust Him enough to follow the path He laid out. God so loved, and then they came toward Him. Any other order would ultimately leave heaven empty, at least of us.

Now we know all this, and we celebrate the good fortune that has become ours because of God's grace. But did you know that loving people like that is part of the mission God handed to us, too? That's right! If we're going to love like Jesus loved, we must love who He loved (previous chapter) and how He loved—first! We can only expect people to find Jesus among us if we act like Jesus did toward us.

> We can only expect people to find Jesus among us if we act like Jesus did toward us.

That means we can't turn up our noses at people just because they stink with sin.

So did we, once. And Jesus loved us in a way that is proving life-changing.

How many times did Jesus live stories of amazing love for us to see? No matter how many known sinners abandoned their old ways, no matter how many women spent a year's wages to lovingly pour perfume on His feet, no matter how many broken, desolate folks found hope, the Pharisees maintained their distance from those who didn't look like them. It's amazing how many still think like those guys today.

Love is the only thing that changes people. It's not the carrot on a stick, the hope of future blessing that comes when we get our act together.

God loves so we can find Him. And if we'll love, we can be a part of that possibility for the damaged folks around us.

This is the Spirit-empowered disciple's greatest moment—to love those who don't know, who don't believe, and who even don't care. That's more than just a love that anticipates nothing in return. It's a love that expects rejection, knowing Christ's servants won't be treated better than the One whose name they carry (John 15:20).

Jesus' love doesn't stop with rejection. He keeps knocking. He took the beatings, the thorns, the nails, and still held His arms out to the ones who pounded them in. And in His moment of colossal agony, He offered grace to one nearby who somehow thought He looked like God right then (Luke 23:42–43).

Can we love like that? Probably not.

But remember what happens when want and need come together. When our desire to be like Him connects with our inability to meet the challenge, God responds with what we need so we can do what He calls us to do. That's why missionaries can weep over those they've yet to meet. That's why bullies find the other cheek so easy to turn. That's why Jesus can say, "Father, forgive them, for they do not know what they are doing" (Luke 23:34). We love first, without condition, and that love reveals the face of God.

Jesus loved you that way, and His plan is to give you the power to join Him in that mission. The more you consider your own experiences of His love, the more willing you become to be that conduit. Freely receive then freely give.

∞

What does the Spirit-empowered life look like? Well, when it comes to connecting with others, it means a deep passion for people, one that can't remain on the sidelines when eternal hope and life are at stake.

It means loving redemptively, knowing there's no greater moment than when faith breaks sin's grip and repentance steals its power. The truth that God offers relationship to all who believe in Him becomes the most critical news of every day and a message worth spending our lives to help spread.

It means we love like Jesus did, stepping over boundaries both real and imagined. Jesus loved those far different from Himself and opened God's door to people from every imaginable background and story.

It means we open our hearts to those who won't open theirs. We love first, just like Jesus did for us. We lay aside our comfortable conditions and embrace those who carry what we have never touched, knowing that only when they find a friend will they turn from their tragic highway and follow that friend toward life.

We can't connect like that without a lot of help, which is exactly why Jesus wants to empower us with His Spirit. We can't and we won't, but He can and He will. And when we long to connect like He does, He'll give us what we need to be more than we've ever been.

That's the shape a Spirit-empowered life begins to take.

THINK ABOUT IT

1. Why is it so difficult to love people before they accept or appreciate you?
2. How does knowing God loved you first help open your eyes to the needs of those around you?
3. What would it look like for you to love people first?

CHAPTER 21

Grow: Doing the Book

S pirit-empowered disciples not only connect with people in remarkable ways, we also make great priority of the Bible—the book that offers both God's history and purposes in this world. While the powerful experiences we encounter provide strong equipping for life, at no point does the Spirit-empowered life reach its maximum potential. <u>Growth, for disciples, is a lifelong journey, defined and guided by the teachings</u> of the Bible. No matter how remarkable the demonstrations of God's power become or how evident we find the anointing of God's Spirit, there is always another step forward. And no matter how many such steps we take, we always remain short of God's unreachable standard, so there is simply no justification for pride . . . ever. The Bible makes that clear.

What is the Bible?

Is it a mere collection of remarkable stories that provides the legends of Judaism and Christianity? Is it a rule book designed to calibrate a moral compass that might guide even modern life? Some have relegated it to such places, deeming the multiple copies that fill their bookshelves as rarely perused reference tools. But those views don't lead to powerful living; rather, they more easily result in the learning and doing approach to Christianity that we know to be inadequate.

The Bible is so much more than that.

Yes, the stories are amazing. Children still sit mesmerized by the exploits of unlikely people, regardless of whether those people dance across a computer screen or stick to a flannel board like they did when their parents were kids. Who hasn't imagined themselves as young David, turning a few skipping stones into missiles that changed the course of a nation? I doubt I'm the only kid who tried to part my own bath water or at least imagine what it might look like if I could. And even the simplest boat ride can conjure images of a great fish beneath that might swallow a man whole and then let him build a campfire in its cavernous belly (at least, that's what my Sunday school papers showed).

But there's more to these stories. The Spirit-empowered life suggests exactly what my childlike faith hoped for. These stories are not just to be read; they are to be lived. The same God who shut the mouths of lions can still tame the big cats today. The Israelites passed down these stories—orally from generation to generation—to stir their faith and help them believe that God was able to help them overcome their current impossible predicaments. We read them and tell them with more than hope. Our thirst is to live them!

The book of Hebrews says that when God speaks, His Word is "alive and active" and slices deep into the hearts of the hearers (Heb. 4:12). This is no static rule book where dust must be routinely blown from its yellowing pages—not for the Spirit-empowered. Rather, the Bible has a remarkable capacity to speak into generations far removed from both the moment and the context of its original writing. So Solomon can offer up wisdom from his ancient palace that guides the daily choices of a cab driver in Brazil. Apostles can write from dimly lit prison cells the truths that speak powerfully to the affluent businessman who looks down from his high-rise office. The book speaks in ways that far outdistance its original moments, and its message proves life-changing.

> Apostles can write from dimly lit prison cells the truths that speak powerfully to the affluent businessman who looks down from his high-rise office.

How can a book be so powerful? The same Spirit that empowers the disciple also spoke into the minds of those who penned its many pages. It's God's Word, not just a big book about God. That's what gives it penetrating power. That's how it both defines and sparks faith.

The Bible speaks to all who will listen. Every child finds the proof of God's love to be captivating. Adults engage its wisdom and nod approvingly at its advice. In fact, the only people who reject this book as useless are those who were predisposed to do so. Even the Bible can't cure a blindness we are determined to hold onto (Matt. 13:14).

The Bible also proves to be highly durable. It can be studied intently and dissected by the most proven scholar and yet provide an easily grasped path of life for the nearly illiterate. How can such a diverse audience find life-changing value in its pages? By learning to do the book.

Believers' lives are shaped by our continuing effort to put the principles and teachings of the Bible into practice. Noting how others responded to their own moments is insufficient by itself. Those stories provide a pattern for response. So we see Simon Peter wrestle to forgive someone repeatedly (Matt. 18:21) and draw out our own compulsion to forgive. When Jesus tells us how to pray, He does so because He wants us to pray, too. In a very real way, the pages come to life because the story is life—and we are in the same story.

Spirit-empowered disciples approach the Bible with expectation. Ours is not a study for devotional meaning alone. Instead, we come to the Bible in search of direction—a life plan—and anticipate that God will use His Word to provide much-needed practical guidance. And we expect similar results. If God responded to the prayers of the ancients with healing, then He may well drive away sickness in the modern moment, too. We expect to find answers, and we expect God to do as He has done.

When we read that young Samuel responded to God's call saying, "Speak, for your servant is listening" (1 Sam. 3:10), we follow his pattern. When we see the apostles place their hands on the sick as they pray, we do so as well. When we read that those filled with God's Spirit spoke in unknown tongues, we look for the same sign. We do what they did because we want what they found.

So Spirit-empowered people live in those pages. They read in order to do, not so they might become their own brand of heroes, but so they might find life on its highest level—the level of connection with and service to God that He intended.

As a moral guide, the Bible becomes necessary. The subjectivity of our own thinking proves that we must have a standard outside of ourselves in order to live a consistent life. It's easy for us to be "black and white" on issues that have yet to affect us, but once we are touched by difficulty or setback, we get a bit lost in the gray areas. So we occasionally change our own rules and justify other paths if we are left to our own definitions of truth.

The Bible doesn't move. As a timeless guide for life, it keeps the sin lists accurate and the promises evident. When I can't be trusted to speak truth because I'm struggling to live my own words, the Bible continues to speak. When I turn from hope because my circumstances have become more than I can manage, the Bible doesn't turn with me. Instead, it paints a consistent path to the joy that "comes in the morning" (Ps. 30:5).

Ultimately, the Bible is God's written revelation of who He is and how the life He created works best. More than wisdom, more than standards, *He can be found there*. Having engaged in relationship with God, Spirit-empowered disciples treasure the pages of the Bible as our best source for understanding and knowing the heart of our eternal Father and Friend. So doing the book becomes a way to walk beside God, to follow where He leads, and to find the path to His individual purpose for our lives.

> Ultimately, the Bible is God's written revelation of who He is and how the life He created works best.

Jesus said, "If you love me, keep my commands" (John 14:15).

Not only do we find God's path and even His character in the pages of the Bible, we also find the means of demonstrating our love for Him. Jesus Himself tagged the greatest commandment as: "Love the Lord your God with all your heart and with all your soul and with all your mind" (Matt. 22:37). Most Christ-followers know those words, but how can they live the words? It's not easy to hug God. Who can get their arms around Him?

Instead, Jesus showed us that obedience is the path to such expression. Like the child considering whether or not to heed a parent's words with his next action, we prove love through obedience. What an extraordinary combination—God loves us enough to guide us with His wisdom, and we love Him back by following the path He lays out. Seems easy enough, doesn't it?

Yet, there's often a battle between what we want to do and what we end up choosing (Rom. 7:15). Paul called it a war between flesh and Spirit, and admitted that he didn't always land on the right side. The Spirit-empowered life isn't simply one of determined obedience; instead, it's a constant recognition that we must have God's help and the power of His Spirit to fuel our obedience.

God won't make us automatons. He won't override our wills and our choices, but He will fuel the choices we make. Again, want and need merge and find the experience of His power exactly what we need to follow our, or actually His, heart.

Too many Christians hope that God will make them more obedient. They confront their areas of struggle by waiting for God to obliterate their fleshly desires and herd them down the right path. Now, God has occasionally drained the taste for evil from the lips of the sincere, but His more common plan is to wait for their initial steps of repentance (turning away from sin). Then He motorizes those steps with His power. They choose, and He delivers the strength they need to live those choices.

There is no Spirit-empowered life apart from the truth of God's Word. Those who experience God's power find themselves on a collision course with His revealed truth. They live the book—even in those places where they may never have held one in their hands.

THINK ABOUT IT

1. What are some of the ways that God has guided you through the words of the Bible?
2. What are some of the Bible's commands that you find difficult—maybe even impossible—to live?

CHAPTER 22

Grow: Expecting God to Speak

There may be no idea more puzzling and potentially dangerous among the Spirit-empowered than the thought that God speaks into life's moments. Indeed, some have misused and even abused such claims in order to manipulate others or add supernatural weight to their own sense of direction. To say, "God told me . . . " instantly elevates what follows to a potential authority that's difficult to argue against.

Yet, God does speak, and He speaks to the Spirit-empowered.

As we consider how the Spirit-empowered life grows and is expressed in discipleship, we can't dismiss a key ingredient to the uniqueness of such a life: The same God who offers relationship does some of the talking, too.

Wow! First, let's allow that to sink in.

Would the God who manufactured the universe with mere sentences and has, thus far, generated more than 20 billion unique expressions of human life actually take time to converse with one of those little characters? Given that He's designed a specialized path for each of those little characters and shows up to aid us in our daily struggles, the idea isn't too far-fetched, is it?

Does God really speak? Apparently He did.

The Bible says He had conversations with the first couple, chatting them up "in the cool of the day" (Gen. 3:8). My wife and I greatly enjoy the covered porch on the back of our house. We know when the "cool of the day" occurs in our part of the world, and that porch is the best place to spend it. Comfortable chairs, overhead fans, and the best possible view of the yard we've worked hard to maintain. Apparently God visited Adam and Eve's back porch.

God spoke to Noah, too—turned his flower beds into a shipyard. It's hard to imagine building such a massive boat far from any waterways. I guess you just tell people that God said to do it . . . and they end up thinking you're crazy!

Imagine Abram explaining to his parents why he was leaving the family ranch and heading, literally, God knew where (Gen. 12:1). People simply didn't strike out on their own in those days without friends or family waiting at the end of the journey. "God told me . . . " probably sounded a bit weird and doubtful in that family meeting, too.

We could go on. Again and again, the biblical authors convey moments of God's direction with the idea that God spoke to their story's main character, so he or she obeyed. Sometimes it comes across as so matter of fact that you miss the likely awkwardness of the original moment.

Nothing sounds worse than when God doesn't speak. Even those who can't imagine what it would be like for God to speak can agree that a silent God doesn't sound good. But for four centuries, God's voice disappeared from among His people. No prophets announced God's plans or even underlined their failures. Nobody heard His voice. No wonder Bethlehem's big night caught everyone by surprise. When God finally spoke again, it was in the gurgling of an infant—an event so important it recalculated our calendars.

> God speaks, and it seems unlikely to think He doesn't. After all, how could He call our connection a relationship if He remained silent and aloof?

God speaks, and it seems unlikely to think He doesn't. After all, how could He call our connection a relationship if He remained silent and aloof? Some think that God's days of speaking are long past—"He doesn't do that anymore"—as if writing down what He said centuries ago would be sufficient for a living relationship now. *No, mom, I'm not calling anymore. Just keep rereading my baby book and playing those VHS tapes of our earliest conversations . . .*

That wouldn't be much of a relationship, would it?

Prayer would take on a helpless feeling if there were no hope of response. Our one-sided droning would resemble the meaningless chants of those who worship non-existent gods. Remember that Elijah endured a whole day of false prophets trying to get a stone image to animate and sprinkle fire on their sacrifices (1 Kings 18:25–29). Their futility is comical, though their wicked intent was not. If God didn't speak or respond to our prayers, wouldn't that be us?

Yet many modern Christians live with no expectation that God will respond to their prayers. They recite words from their childhood, occasionally adding some adult sentences to prove their achieved maturity, but they stopped listening for a response long ago. Little wonder a pastor's effort to compel them to daily prayer rarely gets off the ground. Other than telling God what He already knows, what could happen?

And then someone crosses our path saying, "God told me" to do this or that, to go here or there, and we recoil with eyebrows askew and don our most skeptical pose. The claim clumsily bumps into our suspicion, and our heart walls lock into place. *God doesn't do that,* we think, though we're usually too polite and maybe a bit too unsure to say it out loud.

Now, most of us want God to talk to us, but we don't want to throw His name around either. His is the ultimate name to drop, and doing so to gain someone's attention to our own ideals sounds a lot like taking that name in vain—one of the top ten "don'ts" we know so well. And yes, there have been those who seem unconcerned with misusing His name. Recently, a commercial for a Christian computer dating service told me what God wants me to do, but my wife would hardly agree. I think there's good reason to question their claim of God speaking, especially since their corporate balance sheet is the most likely beneficiary.

But God does speak, often loudly and clearly, too.

We know that God speaks through the Bible. That book is the collection of a lot of things He has already spoken. And what God has said still has a great deal of application to our modern relationships with Him.

Spirit-empowered people frequently hear God's voice through those things He has spoken to past disciples. When Jesus encouraged His band of followers, "Do not be afraid" (Luke 12:32), Spirit-empowered disciples through the ages have taken courage. When He told His friend Martha to "believe" as they walked toward her brother Lazarus's tomb (John 11:26), we take heart in our painful moments and tingle with expectancy as we anticipate what He is about to do. Promises echo through the centuries and speak to our matching moments as though uttered just for us.

While the Bible exudes the voice of God for all of us, it doesn't represent the sum total of that voice. Indeed, God speaks even when chapter and verse can't be found.

These are the "God told me . . . " experiences many people view with suspicion. A friend says, "God told me to call you" as she expresses concern for your predicament. Another says, "God told me to stop the car, and seconds later someone in need wandered by." Still others are awakened in the night, overwhelmed with an urgent desire to pray for a distant friend, only to later discover they had been awakened at the exact hour of an unexpected crisis. Are we ready to label these as mere fortuitous coincidences, or can we believe God whispered direction to one who was listening?

Given how full the Bible is of God guiding His people in such ways, wouldn't it be more unusual if such occasions had ceased? How else might God direct those committed to His purposes? Some might think God would have ceased speaking by now, but they likely have other reasons for such thoughts.

In the Spirit-empowered life, disciples must learn to hear God's voice. Rarely does it have an audible quality. Instead, most describe the voice as an impression, an innate sense to move in a certain direction or engage a surprised passerby. Once, I felt a strong urging to speak to an apparently homeless man who had chosen one of my favorite park benches for his bedroom. Somehow it seemed I was supposed to tell him that God saw him and heard him, but that hardly sounded like a typical greeting. *He'd more likely want lunch money*, I thought as I fingered the five-dollar bill in my pocket. That made more sense, but I couldn't escape the inexplicable need to say, "God sees you and hears you," regardless of how awkward it seemed.

> In the Spirit-empowered life, disciples must learn to hear God's voice.

Now, I'm not the outgoing type. I'm more comfortable with words coming out of my fingers (like these) than I am launching them from my mouth, but I couldn't turn away. So I brushed my hand lightly against his shoulder and waited for his eyes to open. When they did, and it took a bit for them to focus, I said my piece and wondered what he would think.

I'd barely finished my sentence when tears appeared in the corners of his eyes and raced each other toward his beard.

"Did God tell you to say that?" The man spoke in a voice that had apparently been unused for about a day.

"Yeah, I think so," I responded, gaining confidence as I saw the impact of my words.

For the next few moments, he told me pieces of his tragic tale, especially the most recent events that had him ready to give up. In fact, just that night, maybe five hours before I began my early morning prayer walk through that park, he had told God that if He cared about him at all . . . well, God would have to prove it because the evidence was pointing the other direction.

So when he woke up to the words I now knew God had told me to say, he had his answer. And with it came a dose of hope he hadn't seen in awhile. I pulled the five-dollar bill from my pocket, but he waved it away. "You've already given me everything I need," he said, with a more than satisfied smile.

Though I sat on that bench every Tuesday morning for the next five years, I never saw him again.

Does God speak? You bet He does, and Spirit-empowered people know it, though we may find it difficult to explain. Most often, that voice issues the command to "step up" and engage an opportunity. *This is your moment*, the voice seems to whisper and implores us toward something we don't feel equipped to achieve.

It had to be the same voice that urged Simon Peter to step toward a lame man on the temple steps. By now, most of Peter's arrogance hung limp against his heart. But when he saw the crippled man, something inside (or more likely Someone) said, "Walk toward him."

Seconds later the once-clumsy disciple said, "Silver or gold I do not have, but what I do have I give you. In the name of Jesus Christ of Nazareth . . ." (Acts 3:6). The rest is remarkable history.

God speaks, and His disciples learn to listen. We're not perfect at it by any means, but like Jesus said, "My sheep listen to my voice" (John 10:27). And the more we hear that voice, the easier it becomes to step out in faith.

God has the words for us to say and the power we'll need to speak strength into crippled legs. He does the heavy lifting, but He chooses to use us as His delivery drivers. And it's an amazing moment every time He does.

THINK ABOUT IT

1. What do you think when people say that God has spoken to them? How do you know if He really has?
2. When do you feel God has spoken to you? What did He say, and what did you do?
3. What are some biblical tests that we can apply to experiences of God speaking to us or to others?

23

Grow: Signs to Follow

There are moments when I want to be one of Jesus' original disciples, living in the amazing events that routinely arose on their paths across the Judean countryside. I want to be there as He teaches, to see His eyes of compassion as He heals the sick, and to wave pompoms as He tackles Pharisaical accusations with words that hit like a linebacker. Those would be days that light up the Twitter account and make for some impressive Facebook posts.

This was not one of those days.

There are days when I'm glad for the two-thousand-year distance between me and Jesus' daily events. I'm glad I missed those late-night boat rides. I know I would have preferred to stay back when the demon-possessed came running toward the group, and I don't think I would have wanted to be there on the day when Jesus suggested that His guys manufacture the impossible.

One fella quickly pointed out that a year's wages couldn't buy Happy Meals for the hungry hordes on that hillside (John 6:7). And none of them was carrying around a year's wages anyway. Jesus is the impossible-moments specialist, but He seems to have been passing that responsibility to the unprepared in this story. That's why I'm glad I wasn't there.

You probably know the story. The disciples gathered up the available food and only found a boy's lunch among a crowd of more than five thousand men (v. 9). I guess that says a lot about how prepared men can sometimes be, but their wives hadn't done any better. So upwards of ten thousand people needed food and nobody had any—except a kid whose mother seems to be the only person who saw this crisis coming.

So, the disciples organized the throng into smaller groups and they all sat down, licking their lips in anticipation of the bread crumbs they might be fortunate to taste.

Then things got interesting. Jesus started breaking bread and tossing it into baskets. He slapped a filet in there too, then another, and . . . uh, another.

Bartholomew grabbed the first basket, stunned at how heavy it felt. *How did that kid carry it, and how did he get all of this in his little basket? Hmm . . .*

Soon the disciples' voices rose with excitement as they realized what was happening. Fish came out of baskets faster than fishermen had ever pulled them from nets. Bread, and more bread, and even more bread filled each container to the rim, and no matter how fast Bartholomew distributed it to the thousand or so people in his area, the basket never emptied.

After an hour of eating like many hadn't eaten in weeks, the baskets were brought back to Jesus full. Bartholomew was too stuffed to look at another piece of bread, but he knew that even if he filled his arms with a dozen more loaves, nothing would empty that basket. There would always be more!

Okay, that would have turned out to be a good day to hang out with the disciples after all. If ever there had been a moment that proved Jesus was more than just a remarkable teacher, that had to be it. Surely now the people would believe God had sent Him. Bartholomew sure did.

But they didn't.

In fact, the next day the crowds gathered again, but this time Jesus seemed frustrated. Had they come back because they now believed His message, or were they in line for more food? The question hung in the air too long for the disciples to feel good about the answer.

That's the problem with miracles. They offer overwhelming evidence that Someone beyond the norm is present and that something is happening that demands close attention. Yet those who observe or experience them often end up swamped by self-satisfaction and the need for even more. Sensationalism overtakes the sensational.

> God has called us to relationship, not where every hunger pang finds a hunk of fish, but where faith and trust become products of an even deeper connection.

Most of us have had our moments of thinking, *If only someone were healed at our church, the place would be packed.* I suppose attendance would increase, at least for a while, but would faith join it a few steps higher on the ladder? Not always.

That's why miracles alone can't get the job done. God has called us to relationship, not where every hunger pang finds a hunk of fish, but where faith and trust become products of an even deeper connection.

Still, the miraculous has a way of drawing a crowd and offering evidence that God is in the house. That's why Jesus' days were filled with miracles. Yes, it's great to alleviate suffering. If you've ever been in crisis, you know you would take a miracle in a heartbeat. The relief can be life-changing.

But Jesus' miracles had a deeper purpose. He intended this supernatural evidence to demonstrate that He had come from a supernatural place. No tricks, no natural explanations. God had come to people, offering proof in baskets of food, restored eyesight, and vanishing skin diseases. So they lined up with their needs, and Jesus obliged them with the greatest slate of the miraculous ever seen on planet Earth. Better than Moses, more amazing than Samuel, and far more than Elijah ever thought about doing. These signs sent a message to all who would see them—God is with us.

This strategy of divine revelation would continue. Jesus promised that as amazing as His own works had been, His disciples would do even more. "Greater things" (John 14:12) He called them, underscoring an anticipated explosion of God moments that would soon sweep the Middle East and beyond. And they did.

But where are they now? The blind show up at church and return home again, tapping their sticks before them. The broken hear words of hope, but nothing changes. Healings are remembered, even as those who remember them die of a disease. If this is the church, chasing after the same Savior who fed thousands, where has all the power gone?

In the same passage that Simon Peter quoted on the day of Pentecost, he described generations like ours as belonging to the last days. Is there no cause for announcing God's kingdom in this final era? The Bible indicates ours as a time of great expectation, but the reality rarely matches. Those who've decided such days are past seem content with the experience of yesterday, but surely this isn't God's plan.

He wants more, and the Spirit-empowered share that same passion.

Across the globe, peoples' need of God is routinely punctuated by the supernatural. Healings, deliverances, and amazing provision more than dot the distant landscape. But those here at home live with little expectation and even less experience of God's power. Perhaps the stories of others are meant to suffice for us, but that doesn't seem likely, does it?

Our hunger for God's power offers a more likely cause. Until we want more and are desperate enough to pursue our great need, it seems God will allow our self-styled religion to rule the day until it wastes away. We can fill arenas, but our capacity to empty hospitals needs some work.

Imagine what could be. The sparkling gold of God's transforming power in hands of clay like ours. Marriages once dissolved beyond repair now clinging together with unimagined strength. Our leprosies, often more internal than worn just under the sleeve, dissolved into pink, healthy tissue without the trace of a scar. And the destitute that number among the affluent? Picture them singing as they carry baskets of bread and fish to their homes. Better yet, picture the affluent carrying those baskets for them.

Some insist that miracles should no longer be needed in a Christian nation. Surely God has done enough among us to make His point. More miracles would just make us lazy. Our abundance is miracle enough to underscore God's goodness. Perhaps that's true, but there may never have been a time when the Western world needed proof of God more than now. Rationalism has melted into self-dependence in a way that has scholars writing off the supernatural stories of the Bible. Postmodernism has vaulted into the national spotlight as a new generation interprets their parents' godless behavior to mean there really isn't a God. Wouldn't now be as good a time as any for supernatural proof of One who offers more?

What could God be waiting on?

Perhaps the answer is exactly where the Spirit-empowered disciple might expect to find it—a lack of want and need coming together amidst the economically comfortable. As long as the life we're making for ourselves seems to be functioning satisfactorily, is there any room for spiritual desperation? Can want and need truly rise if we can manufacture what we want and pretend we have no need? Until hunger for truth replaces the slate of our own inadequate answers, it seems unlikely that miracles could ever produce faith—no, they'd just offer short-lived headlines.

> God has promised to empower us, just as He does others, but we must return to doing things His way.

Now is the time for Spirit-empowered living.

One can hardly argue that God is less willing to reveal Himself to this generation or that He somehow prefers to connect with those other than us. On the contrary, if the real culprit is our self-dependence and smug strategies to resource ourselves, then the fault is in our plan, not His. And the answer would be within our grasp as well.

We must return to kingdom priorities and recognize that our satisfaction with mere learning and doing isn't satisfying at all. God has promised to empower us, just as He does others, but we must return to doing things His way.

When Jesus prepared to send His disciples into their mission fields, He did so with the promise of power—signs and wonders that would follow them everywhere they went (Mark 16:17). They would follow Christ and signs would follow them. That order is significant.

You see, many modern Christians imagine that if God would just show them a sign or perform some miraculous event, their commitment would skyrocket and others would likely come running. *C'mon, Jesus, make something big happen and watch what we'll do then!*

It's a great idea, but the wrong order.

Jesus said that signs will follow as we obey His Commission. As we go, He will prove that He is with us, even leading us forward. So when we encounter brokenness, our desire and need for His help open the way for Him to do just that. We're not supposed to have the answers for suffering. We've been equipped by the One who is the answer! And He'll prove that as we lean on Him for our next step. Do it yourself and God will let you. Hunger for Him and admit you can do nothing on your own, and you won't have to.

Remember, God wants to reveal Himself far more than you want Him to be seen. And He will prove His presence in ways more powerful than you can imagine. The Spirit-empowered life doesn't make things happen but knows that God stands ready and willing to prove Himself to a generation that no longer believes He is there.

THINK ABOUT IT

1. Why do you think people want to see miracles more than they want to know God?

2. Why do you suppose Jesus said the signs would "follow" those who believe?

3. How can the miraculous "punctuate" your message? What does the miracle reveal about you? About God?

Grow: Teach
Them to Obey

G o make disciples." The command hangs in the air compelling every follower of Christ toward a mission greater than ourselves. More than a call to the committed, Jesus' commissioning words come as a mandate to every one of us—a mandate many fail to engage.

By definition, a mandate is a command from a superior court or official to a lower one. It's an order, a directive one has been empowered to achieve and is expected to carry out. In that sense, it's difficult to think the assignment is optional for any who have laid claim to eternal salvation. Quite simply, this is what Jesus saved us to do.

Many a church leader has said that we are in the "people" business. (We even said that a few chapters ago.) That's true to a point. Our work is with people and for people, but our true business is also to achieve the specific target of helping people become disciples. Mere "people" business could have us chasing many different initiatives that involve human beings. Many organizations work the "people" business with differing motives and goals. Ours is singular and clear—we make disciples.

Do we? How do each of us engage this particular mission? How do you? Do we perceive our partnership with others at church as our primary contribution to the cause? Is our pastor the disciple-maker we pay from our worship giving while we pursue our own lives and, hopefully, take care of our own discipleship? Some of us don't even do that much, believing our pastor bears the responsibility for making disciples out of us, too. Given that you're chasing a Spirit-empowered life, I'm confident that you're not one of those.

But how are *we* making disciples?

In the modern church, disciple-making has become a bit complex. The "learning and doing" model of Christian living has loaded bookstore shelves with thousands of possible options. And some have given discipling elaborate and complicated definitions or offered various checklists of topics and action steps. Honestly, at times, the journey feels almost as overwhelming as registering for your first semester at a university. People start their journey of faith with too many books in their arms and panicked looks on their faces as they try to find the right building in a maze of massive, ivy-covered structures.

I don't think Jesus intended discipling people to be that hard. Frankly, the level of today's current complexity would quickly surpass those original disciples. Their efforts seem more practically focused, where the sandal meets the road. They lived something that was remarkably effective and might teach us a thing or two.

They listened to what Jesus said—and just did that.

> What Jesus wants each of us to do is to teach others what He has taught us.

You see, Jesus defined making disciples when He said it was about "teaching them to obey everything I have commanded you" (Matt. 28:20). Okay, let's get this straight. What Jesus wants each of us to do is to teach others what He has taught us. So I help a friend learn what I have learned, I pass along what my recent challenge taught me about God, and maybe someone shares what he or she has learned from me.

That's making disciples? I can do that.

This definition of discipling sounds familiar, doesn't it? It's that "freely receive, freely give" idea. Once again, Jesus doesn't ask us to give anything except what He has already given to us. So the hard lessons I learned in my last effort to forgive aren't just for my benefit and my private diary. I can share them with others, maybe even giving them the chance to skip over the painful experience themselves as they learn from mine. Just teaching others what we have learned is a mandate everyone can engage, no matter how much we have learned so far.

That's what Spirit-empowered disciples do. Yes, there is value in deep scholarship. We need folks to help us find the greater treasures of Scripture. And yes, there's value in the efforts of some to organize great educational approaches to the Bible so we don't miss any of its available truths. But real discipleship is one Christ-follower sharing a lesson learned over cups of coffee with another. So being a "witness" is simply sharing what I've seen, heard, and experienced of Jesus, and making disciples means telling someone else what Jesus has been teaching me. That sounds like a mandate even uneducated fishermen can engage.

In a sense, making disciples is reproducing ourselves. Now we're not attempting to clone our spiritual experience. God's unlimited creativity is demonstrated in the unique life journeys He has for each one of us. Some religious leaders have sought to control their followers, limit their influences, and dictate their decisions. That may seem like reproducing oneself, but it's not making disciples. It's making more of that individual, which is not the plan.

When parents reproduce themselves into the life of a child, there's certainly some shared DNA. In certain ways the child looks like Mom and acts like Dad, but no one would call that child a clone. The boy has his own personality, his own interests. Though highly influenced by the parents who "produced" him, he will grow into something else. Nurture can't conquer the uniqueness of nature. (If you think your child is your clone, have another one and you'll see my point.)

> When we share our lives and reproduce faith in others, we may have a significant influence on them.

When we share our lives and reproduce faith in others, we may have a significant influence on them. They may think and act a bit like us, at least for a while, but their own unique traits and the nurture of their own slate of experiences will ultimately prove them to be more than us. We don't reproduce ourselves, we make disciples.

Now here's where I might explain how to get started, but you probably don't need that. Your journey of making disciples has already begun. It began when Jesus started making one out of you. Just open the book of your life lessons to someone else. Give that person access to where you've been. Share the scrapbook of your journey with Christ, and point out both the high and low points.

And be sure to open yourself to the life lessons others have gained. That's why your church offers classes or small groups—so you can encounter truths discovered along someone else's path. That's how you grow in your life and faith. Don't miss the great wealth of understanding that's stacked up all around you.

That's what the Spirit-empowered person knows. God has already given us everything we need for today, and if He hasn't, He will—just in time for our need. Ours is a simple journey of relationship and experiences, where the One we walk with hands us the items we need when we need them. I don't have to find tomorrow's answers today or generate the strength for my future challenges. He knows what I need and will provide it for me as I need it.

When the disciple makes disciples, he not only helps others learn what he's learned, he also passes along his sense of want and need. To make disciples, we can't just share lists of truth. We also must teach others to crave God's presence and purpose and never to forget their ongoing need for God's help and power. To reproduce Spirit-empowered disciples, we must help them walk a similar path of hunger and need. The task of making disciples isn't simply information download. These new friends must experience God's power for themselves. Such was the priority of those early disciple makers, and it can't be less important to us.

Spirit-empowered disciples know that our part is to want God's help and to know that without that help, failure is inevitable. I can't live this life without God providing and equipping me every step of the way. I want Him and I need Him, and that's when He gladly empowers me with capacity greater than my own.

The Spirit-empowered life proves itself in a commitment to grow. There's always a "next level" to attain, a deeper connection with God and His truth to explore. These disciples demonstrate that desire with a close adherence to the Bible. We know that Book is God's written revelation of Himself and His purposes, and we seek to connect it to our lives by doing what it demonstrates.

The Spirit-empowered also learn to hear God's voice. We know that He will speak words of direction to help us see opportunities others might miss. We know He's ready to reveal His power in places of need. Miracles occur among the Spirit-empowered, not because of our skill or capacity but because God desires to demonstrate His presence among us. The Spirit-empowered long to see Him revealed, and their understanding of how they need Him never ceases to grow.

Ultimately, Spirit-empowered disciples know we live under a mandate— to make disciples. Jesus commands us to teach what we've been taught and to let our own experiences be a curriculum for coaching and encouraging others, just as we gain insight and help from their stories.

Spirit-empowered people grow. Every day, we seem to move further from the futility of what we once were while on a path of becoming more like Jesus. Some lessons come harder than others, and the temptation to regress or even give up occasionally revisits even those who have come far down the path. But in the end, we know that every moment, even the most difficult, will work together for our good and our continued growth.

THINK ABOUT IT

1. Who has played a key role in you becoming and growing as a disciple? Who have you helped in a similar way?
2. How can sharing your own journey and the lessons you have learned be helpful and even necessary for others who want to know Christ?
3. How important is it to understand the life lessons you share through the teachings of the Bible?

CHAPTER 25

Serve: This Is Growing

Jesus had a unique way of looking at the people in a room. On one occasion, He stood with His disciples as people placed offerings into the temple treasury (Mark 12:41). While the disciples gawked at the familiar scene of high-ranking religious types making a production out of their contributions, Jesus' eyes were elsewhere: on a widow who was giving all she had. Hers was a sacrifice of love, and perhaps last hope, as her few coins tumbled into the receptacle.

In other settings, Jesus saw people we often overlook, too. We tend to watch those who dominate a room, whose very presence captures attention. Surely they are where the action is. The ideas they express and the plans they make are the ones that will affect political direction and pocketbooks. They are the important people whose every breath seems to blow the waves of society.

But Jesus wouldn't be looking at them. Instead, He would focus on others—the servants in the room. Jesus sees those who fill water glasses and says they are great, perhaps even the greatest under the roof.

Why? How is it that our well-honed sense of honor and greatness could differ so much from His? We work hard to climb those hills. We know that the highest ranking spots are reserved for the most talented, the most dedicated, and the ones with the most stuff. Our rooms are well-organized, pecking order in place, and the ones Jesus is watching don't even make our list.

But they make His; in fact, they land at the top. Maybe His preference reveals His love for the underdog. Maybe He looks forward to the day the tables will be turned and the forgotten prove memorable. Maybe He's just anti-whatever those big names might be.

Actually, the reason hits closer to home: a servant recognizes other servants. Jesus came, not to be served, but to serve the deepest needs of those He created (Matt. 20:28). So it's no surprise that He would have His eye on those who know they are called to serve as well. In God's kingdom, things often seem upside down when compared to the thinking that surrounds us. Actually it's more likely that our mentality has been flipped the wrong way. His way is truth.

Jesus' disciples struggled with this particular issue—much as we do. They wrestled with each other for places of prominence. With the buzz of a coming kingdom, even the mother of James and John couldn't resist arguing for preferred spots for her boys who had sacrificed their places in the family fishing business.

> In God's kingdom, things often seem upside down when compared to the thinking that surrounds us.

Against the backdrop of her request, Jesus made the point that "whoever takes the lowly position" gets the title of "greatest in the kingdom of heaven" (Matt. 18:4). I can almost picture the guys racing for the water pitchers. "Here, Jesus, let me get you some grapes. If this is how you get the best spot, then I'll show you I can carry a tray with the best of them!"

But the feeling didn't seem to last long. In fact, on their final night together—the same night Jesus was betrayed—it was Jesus who grabbed a water basin and started washing feet. Now that was awkward. Peter expressed everyone's embarrassment when he tried to refuse. He pulled his feet under his tunic saying to Jesus, "You shall never wash my feet" (John 13:8). In the continuing conversation, Jesus offered more pointed teaching on the subject of servanthood, but it's hard to miss the obvious—no one took the basin or offered to finish the job!

They didn't get it, and we usually don't grasp this idea either. There's something in our nature that prefers the receiving side of the hors d'oeuvre tray. We believe status gives us value, that our thirst for significance can only be slaked by the attention others give us. But Jesus showed us a different way, and given His eternal perspective, it makes sense for us to listen.

You see, we are following a God who serves.

How could we treasure the front seat when the One we are following takes a lesser place? How awkward to pass our water glass only to discover that Jesus is filling it. That's not the way we show gratitude to the One who died for us. It's His agenda that we serve, His kingdom that becomes our focus. Serving Him is our greatest desire, and He says we do that best when we serve others.

Our struggles shouldn't be too surprising, but we soon figure out that serving is growing. In this journey of following Jesus, the act of serving offers more growth potential than just about any other step we can take. Of course, the desire to be served still shows up a lot, too. People connect with churches by the thousands, but only a few are quick to offer help. In most congregations, around 20 percent of the people seem to be doing 80 percent of the work, while the others have yet to learn the personal benefit in serving. Sadly, many of these same folks confront such busy schedules there's no time to serve in other settings either. Life becomes limited to learning and doing, and the exhaustion seems ever present. A pastor's plea for help sounds like one more thing to do in a life with too many things already.

Many of these same folks describe their Christian journey as stagnant and boring. They continue to attend church because it's good for the kids, but sleeping in on Sunday morning sure sounds appealing. Though their church offers many attractive experiences, these struggling friends inch closer to deciding their life of faith has seldom proved life-changing. They need the growth that only serving can bring.

> It is in serving that you discover your true gifts. You discover talent and abilities.

Serving others opens you to amazing possibilities. It is in serving that you discover your true gifts. You discover talent and abilities. You know what you're good at, even if you're reluctant to admit such information to others.

But serving uncovers gifts, not just talents. When you serve God, you find capacity no one knew you possessed, including yourself. That's why God could find His future king for Israel strumming a harp and singing praise ditties to an audience of sheep. That's why God could uncover a mighty warrior, hiding in a cave and hoping no one would steal his last few kernels of corn. That's why Jesus could give an impetuous and unstable guy named Simon a nickname like "Rock." I can almost hear his brother, Andrew, chuckling at that one.

Who you are and what you were meant to be aren't yet the same. In fact, you possess possibilities you can't even imagine. There are weapons in your arsenal you don't know you have. Only as you serve does God bring them to the surface. They're His gifts—so much more than mere talents or proven abilities.

Some offer elaborate tests to help you figure out your best place to serve, but these can only measure what you want to do, what you've done, and what others have seen you doing. They can't get deeper into your heart to see what God might be up to. He has a way of bringing surprising things to the surface, the kind of things that reveal His presence and power.

That's why Spirit-empowered people often demonstrate unexpected and extraordinary gifts. Normal people doing abnormal things. When a carpenter's kid in a small, impoverished community turns out to be God, there must be a lot of other surprises ahead.

Serving also drives the other elements of spiritual growth. When I'm doing something for God's purpose, my own connection to Him stays on the front burner. I pray more. I value the truths I'm learning from His Word more deeply. I remain more aware of my need for His help, and that puts me in a place to experience the Holy Spirit's help and power.

Jesus spent several afternoons on hillsides in teaching settings, but the majority of His efforts to make disciples out of His followers occurred "on the street." Theirs was an active curriculum where the lessons He offered connected them with real people and with real needs. Following Jesus wasn't a textbook experience. It was a life lived in the marketplace of human struggle.

Why was Jesus' class on a perpetual field trip? Because serving provided the best form of on-the-job training. Parables provided truth that crowds could put into practice. His truth was to be lived by His disciples so it could prove to be life-changing for the people they met. And in the midst of such moments, they found His true heart and purpose.

It makes sense that a God who loves and serves would put His disciples in those same opportunities. That's the only place where they could experience His heart. What sentence of truth could speak as loudly as watching Jesus reach toward the broken with compassion? What book could teach what His tenderness and power could demonstrate? They saw His passion, they came to know His priorities, and they spent the rest of their lives following His example.

That's how the Spirit-empowered life is revealed in serving. God has placed His Spirit in us, and He wants us to become the hands and feet to His heart. We move toward people with a desire to care for them because the One who dwells within us would move in that same direction.

Spirit-empowered disciples serve. It's in our new nature. We don't worry about attention and popularity in this life, knowing we have God's full attention and will celebrate His kingdom throughout eternity.

Those who won't serve have yet to encounter the true life-change He offers. And those who serve without His power will find their strength insufficient for much of that road. There's only one way to do His work, and that is by His Spirit (Zech. 4:6). And there's only one way to live once that power has come, and that is to give ourselves for the good of even the weakest folks we find.

THINK ABOUT IT

1. Why is serving necessary for believers to understand the heart and purposes of Christ?
2. How has serving others affected you? Has it helped you to grow or shown you the need for God's Spirit and power?

CHAPTER
26

Serve: Motivated by Love

After his horrific night of failing Jesus three times, and then watching—likely from a distance—as Jesus was brutally killed, Peter wasn't feeling too great about his place in Jesus' kingdom. Now, after the resurrection, Peter surely was glad for the miracle, but his future remained unknown. So at the beginning of John 21, we read that Peter decided to go fishing, to return to what he knew and hopefully couldn't mess up.

Thankfully, Jesus wasn't done with His sometimes challenging friend. After interrupting Peter's fishing expedition—yet again—Jesus began to restore the fisherman's hope of a place in His kingdom. "Do you love me?" Jesus asked three times (see John 21:15–17). At first, the question gave Peter a much-needed chance to proclaim his dedication to Jesus once again. But by the third time Jesus asked, the memories of failing three times proved they were still raw. Could he undo such public failure with three private declarations of commitment? Perhaps so, but it probably felt unlikely. Still, before the chapter ends, everything was moving forward again for the fisherman.

But there's more here than restoration. Jesus, it seems, took Peter deeper into an understanding of what He wanted him to do. Fish were no longer on the menu; sheep were the target. With each yes to His probing question, Jesus stated the new mission. "Feed my lambs. . . . Take care of my sheep. . . . Feed my sheep." And in so doing, He connected the dots between ministry and motive in a way that's critical for future disciples as well.

Serving has never seemed an attractive vocation. No one wants the towel and basin. For Peter and his contemporaries, the idea of a kingdom where they ruled alongside Jesus had lots of appeal. Living under the thumb of Roman domination had pretty well destroyed their taste for lower-level lifestyles. A world where Romans served them sounded like a lot more fun.

Would they really have to give up their hope of being "on top" of their future world? No one wanted to.

But now, Jesus changed the conversation. Servanthood has more than a mission; it also has a motive. We serve, not simply because serving is necessary—you know, "someone must sacrifice so others can benefit." No, there's something more and Jesus revealed it in His three matching directives to Peter's responses. "Peter, do you love Me," really means *Peter, because you love Me, feed My lambs.*

This is the reason we serve. Our love for Christ, flowing from the ever-growing relationship we enjoy with Him, gives meaning to our serving. We do for others because of our love for Him!

> Our love for Christ, flowing from the ever-growing relationship we enjoy with Him, gives meaning to our serving.

Honestly, there's no other motive that works over the long haul.

Some people jump into ministry because they love their assigned tasks. Teaching has become their love, helping their passion, singing their joyous celebration. They thrive on moments where their skills meet needs and their resources make a difference. The thrill of such impact feels as though it will never wear thin . . . but it does.

Teaching becomes a chore, especially when our efforts are criticized. Helping gets old when no one seems to appreciate our efforts. Even singing loses its flavor when our voices no longer bring the attention we crave. Our skills feel abused when there's no end to the need and our resources aren't nearly as unlimited as the requirements. Quite simply, our love for what we do will run out when we don't love it like we used to—*and there will be days like that!*

Others find a motive in love for people. Now, that's a good goal since love is the hallmark of Jesus' people. So we love the children we lead in worship. We love the high school students we work with. We are filled with compassion toward the elderly friends we minister to at the local nursing home. Loving people is a natural by-product of the work Jesus gave us to do—at least it should be.

But children aren't always cute, high school students can drive you crazy, and those dear older saints can be pretty sharp-tongued at times. If our motive is love for those we serve, there will be moments when loving them is extremely difficult. And after we've been mistreated by our target audience a few times, serving them loses its appeal. Many Christians have quit in frustration the same ministry efforts they once longed for.

The issue isn't an evil heart but a misguided motive. While loving our kingdom work and loving the people involved contribute to a wonderful attitude and a great experience, they're insufficient in the motive slot. There's only one motive that endures life's ups and downs: an ever-deepening love for Jesus.

He never fails us. He never gets annoying. The reasons we respond to Him in love never dip or decline. They are always sufficient, always legitimate, and always meaningful. When we serve out of love for Christ, we can endure every other setback or frustration. In fact, the only time love for Christ becomes an inadequate motive for serving Him is when we stop loving Him like we once did—and that makes no sense, does it?

Real serving flows from the relationship we have with Christ. Because we love Him, we willingly lay ourselves down in front of others, sacrificing our resources, and giving our absolute best to accomplish the purposes of Christ's kingdom.

In this way, service becomes an act of worship. We take the gifts God has given, the talents and abilities, the resources, and the capacity to deliver them, and place all of that on the altar, celebrating God's great plan to demonstrate His glory. Ours is a relationship where He is great and we are grateful.

So when our efforts to serve become deficient or our desire wanes, the answer isn't found in guilt, trying harder, or any of the other unhealthy places that

> Our acts of service can never be about us when they are truly done for Him.

commonly rise to the top of a "doing" motivation. Instead, we return to our Source, our relationship with God. That connection must be healthy, growing, and shaping our lives. We run to Him and He restores and renews us. As He does, our strength to serve returns.

Love for Christ as a motivator also makes pride an unattractive and less likely destination. When we are fixated on love for Him, how could we take His place or grab praise for ourselves from our efforts to love Him? Our acts of service can never be about us when they are truly done for Him. That's why someday we'll place heavenly crowns at His feet (Rev. 4:10). Everything they represent was done for Him. All else has been burned away.

Yes, at times people will appreciate our sacrifice for their good. Yes, some will admire the skill with which we deliver our ministry tasks. Learning to do them well seems like an important goal when we are working for One we love. But applause can change our hearts and teach us to see ourselves as more than we are. Logic would say that Christ alone is worthy and the power comes from the Holy Spirit, but the temptations to pride can overcome logic. Only a deepening love for Jesus can protect the Spirit-empowered.

The Spirit-empowered life so greatly exceeds the life of learning and doing on this point. When the right motive is in place, serving becomes less about doing and more about becoming like Him. Doing exhausts every resource, but being thrives in the sacrifice. That's why Paul could speak of joyfully participating in Christ's sufferings (Phil. 3:10). The battered and bruised apostle hadn't lost his mind or changed his favorite colors to black and blue. But he had learned that such sufferings served as badges of love for his Savior.

So where can we serve? Finding those who need to be loved seems like a place that would connect most clearly with the mission. The tasks are secondary to the need for God, and He will equip us as we stand ready to love Him and them. But He can only shape our hearts if we have yielded them to Him. That's why unlikely characters can be found in extraordinary settings doing what previously seemed impossible. They see and they love, and He provides what they need to act as He would.

Too often, we become focused more on the "what" of our service than the "why." We consider our talents and measure them against the assignment. If we see a good "fit," we volunteer and launch our journey of doing, provided the requirement doesn't overwhelm our schedules. Little wonder that such an approach seldom brings the desired result.

Spirit-empowered service runs into the desperate place, knowing that God will provide. Trusting ourselves usually means we won't try until we're convinced we already possess what we need. We shrink in the presence of that kind of uncertainty. But the Spirit-empowered life knows God will always be faithful. We give our best but know that ours is not the total of all available resources.

"Do you love Me?"

If you can imagine Jesus asking you the question He kept asking Peter, be sure that your yes isn't the end of the conversation. There's a mission, a life of service you've been called to. If you can say yes to the question, you'll find the ability to say yes to the mission as well.

THINK ABOUT IT

1. Have you ever become weary in serving people? What do you think was at the core of your feelings?
2. Take a few moments and put your love for Christ in words. Write a paragraph (or even a page) that tells Him about that love.

CHAPTER 27

Serve: Hold the Task Loosely

In one late-night conversation, Jesus compared the Holy Spirit to the wind: "*The wind blows wherever it pleases.*" He went on to say that a listener can "hear its sound, but you cannot tell where it comes from or where it is going. So it is with everyone born of the Spirit" (John 3:8). It's hard to blame Nicodemus for being puzzled by the metaphor. Most modern religious leaders struggle to grasp that one, too.

Yet the Holy Spirit often works differently than we expect. Folks seek to explain His indiscernible purposes with, "The Lord moves in mysterious ways." While explaining little, that phrase reveals God's prerogative to do as He pleases even when we can't connect all the dots.

The Spirit-empowered life is lived in what one friend has called life's "white space." While there are many moments we can understand, some exceed us and call for simple but absolute faith. God is at work with a greater plan than we can fully know. He has both an eternal perspective and a deeper purpose than we can see.

In most football games, the coach who calls the plays sits near the top of the stadium where he can get a bird's-eye view of the entire field. From that vantage point, he sees every movement of the game, including the scrum around the ball and the open opportunities down the field. So he calls the plays from that wide perspective and relays them to those on the field below.

Down on the field, the game looks completely different. It's hard for the runner to see beyond the sizeable tacklers headed his way. The goal line seems to be miles in the distance, especially when he's making little progress forward. The analogy isn't perfect because the coach doesn't always call the right plays, but you get the idea of perspective, don't you?

God's perspective is always eternal. He knows the things that so easily consume us comprise a small part of His forever plan for our lives. He works a deeper agenda, one that makes a greater difference than the "play" we might prefer to run. Lessons learned are more important than the events themselves. Truth discovered and faith developed can prove more valuable than quick exits from those would-be tacklers.

So the Holy Spirit works His own will, and the Spirit-empowered embrace that direction. Things can change suddenly, including where disciples go and what we might be doing. Gifts are given in the moment and often lifted when they no longer fit

> This life we long for holds things loosely and grips relationship with God most tightly.

His purpose. This life we long for holds things loosely and grips relationship with God most tightly.

Philip was among the first servants identified for select duty in the Jerusalem church (Acts 6:5). This new assignment became necessary as the ministries of the church grew. The apostles couldn't manage food distribution and other critical needs while maintaining their focus on teaching and prayer, so they chose Philip and a few others to step in. It's noteworthy that their sole qualification for this task was to be "full of the Spirit and wisdom" (v. 3).

But serving meals to the widows in Jerusalem wasn't Philip's full story. A couple of chapters later, we find him in the middle of a great revival in Samaria. That's significant because apparently the apostles hadn't yet gone to Samaria with their message, but one of those food distributors did. And the results were extraordinary (see 8:4–8). The paralyzed and lame were healed and several demon-possessed were delivered, causing many to believe in Philip's message and his God. In fact, the success was so remarkable that many scholars label Philip the church's first evangelist.

Whether he needed such a label is unclear, but his work did get the attention of the apostles. Peter and John came to Samaria to see what the Holy Spirit was doing through this servant far from home.

> They prayed for the new believers there that they might receive the Holy Spirit, because the Holy Spirit had not yet come on any of them; they had simply been baptized in the name of the Lord Jesus. Then Peter and John placed their hands on them, and they received the Holy Spirit. (Acts 8:15–17)

Once again, the empowering moment came upon people who had already believed and were baptized. These Samaritans had received the power Jesus promised, and they were ready to join the same work given to the apostles.

One can imagine Philip's joy at the sight of his converts being launched into God's purposes, but instead, Philip seems to disappear. In the midst of the excitement in Samaria, the Wind blew a new direction. A few verses later, we're told, "Now an angel of the Lord said to Philip, 'Go south to the road—the desert road—that goes down from Jerusalem to Gaza" (v. 26). As we read on, we meet an important finance minister from Ethiopia who was on his way home from a visit to Jerusalem. Now, his story is important, especially for him and for the Commission he'll soon take to his homeland, but the map shows us something more.

The road from Jerusalem to Gaza headed southwest out of the city while Samaria is more than thirty miles to the north. We clearly see that among the many believers available, Philip certainly wasn't the closest to that road, and one would think he had established an important ministry in the Samaritan revival. But the Holy Spirit had a different plan. He selected Philip for this mission for reasons that may elude us, but that's how the Holy Spirit often orchestrates His strategies. He redirects His servants toward the needs and opportunities He sees arising. In fact, moments after baptizing the Ethiopian, Philip disappeared again, this time turning up in Azotus, a city farther up the Mediterranean coast (v. 40).

The Spirit-empowered disciple holds each assignment loosely, knowing that the Spirit who guides may reveal new steps as He wishes. He is the Lord of His harvest, and as servants, we follow His direction. Our paths may not change as abruptly, or seemingly as frequently, as Philip's did, but servants always stand ready to obey whatever the Master may ask.

> The Spirit-empowered disciple holds each assignment loosely, knowing that the Spirit who guides may reveal new steps as He wishes.

This aspect of the Spirit-empowered life has many implications. First, it means we'e never defined by the work we do. Tasks don't shape our identities, even though we give them our best efforts. Like Philip, who managed widow care in Jerusalem, led evangelistic work in Samaria and on a desert road, and who knows what else after that, the Spirit-empowered allow God to use them in numerous and potentially shifting ways.

For us, that means avoiding the lure of position. While the modern church has various offices necessary for its ministry, we must be careful not to think God's kingdom operates in a workplace paradigm. Servants don't "climb ladders" to increase their authority or prominence over others. They don't crave position and hold tightly to the status it seems to provide. Instead, the Spirit-empowered maintain a servant's mentality, knowing God's plans can require change, new direction, and, at times, a narrower scope of influence.

For Philip, the road led from prominence among a great revival in Samaria, where he worked among hundreds of people, to focus on one man on a desert road. Jesus' own ministry moved from thousands munching fish and bread on a hillside to a much smaller group whose lives He changed forever. When we serve a God who loves every individual, the size of the current crowd can't really matter.

Why wouldn't God's plan seek ever-increasing crowds? Why wouldn't He want His servants to climb as high as possible on the influence meter? While God's ways often elude us, this one isn't that difficult to understand. Our tendency toward pride can be a devastating snare. As we've already seen, the thought that life is about us is tragically unhealthy. It causes some to think the kingdom they're building is their own, though they may use God's name for such purposes. People using God's name for their own vain agendas may be the most dangerous way to violate God's command (Ex. 20:7).

The Spirit-empowered must beware of the lure of position and the danger of "mine." To help prevent such travesty, God shifts us and adjusts our assignments in ways that better fulfill His purposes in the world *and in us*. As such, we often find ourselves moving back and forth between visible and hidden moments. Jesus said that if we are "faithful with a few things," He will "put [us] in charge of many things" (Matt. 25:21). Now specifically, the "in charge" part applies to our future place in Christ's kingdom, but there are times when our influence and visible work for God may grow in this life, too. So our journey of serving has a way of shifting back and forth between the "few" and the "many." Our assignment is to be faithful in both situations.

All believers constantly struggle with pride. One can easily see how this core element of sin would be destructive to a servant. It can lead us to so many failures, from thinking our Master owes us certain blessings to living and acting like masters ourselves. This is the "Gentile-style" of leadership

Jesus spoke about when He explained to His disciples how His kingdom would operate differently.

> You know that the rulers of the Gentiles lord it over them, and their high officials exercise authority over them. Not so with you. Instead, whoever wants to become great among you must be your servant, and whoever wants to be first must be your slave—just as the Son of Man did not come to be served, but to serve, and to give his life as a ransom for many. (Matt. 20:25–28)

The Spirit-empowered yield to the Spirit, not to pride. We accept our assignments, knowing we are participating in an eternal plan where our Master is glorified. Such an attitude leaves no room for self-centered agendas. There's only one kingdom to be built, so I hold my own assignment loosely so I am ready for whatever next step God might have for me.

Now holding loosely doesn't mean we avoid deep relationships or great commitments. We must give ourselves fully to the people and places where God places us. Like we see in Philip, the work at hand is worthy of our best effort. So we engage with wholehearted devotion, knowing that future goodbyes are temporary. Eternity together with Christ and with those we have come to love is the greatest possible reward.

So the Spirit-empowered lay aside our own plans. James even pointed out the futility of such plans, knowing that life in the Spirit requires constant flexibility (James 4:13–17). Instead, we live in ready service—ready to give our best to the current assignment while holding it loosely so God can redirect us as He sees fit.

THINK ABOUT IT

1. Why would it be unhealthy to become too attached to a position or place of ministry?
2. Why do you think God sometimes moves His followers from more visible places to tasks that are hidden?

CHAPTER 28

Serve: The Greatest
Serve People

Jesus repeatedly pleaded with His disciples to "lift up their eyes," to get their focus off of themselves or their current challenge to see what He saw every day—people. Only when they saw the faces before them could they develop the right heart for the work He wanted them to do. *If they would just look!*

We have the same struggle.

Men have a strong tendency to become so task-oriented they lose sight of the "who" of ministry effort. Women are typically more relationally sensitive, but the doing can also overtake them at times. We want to serve God, so "doing" easily becomes the primary path.

And there's plenty to do. Hunger needs abating, sickness requires care, and brokenness demands hope and better answers. *If we just had more people we could get more done*, we imagine, knowing all the while that the needs around us will never diminish. I've never wondered how Jesus started a healing line, but I don't know how He could stop one. It seems the more we do, the more we discover needs to be done.

When Jesus spoke of His disciples' future leadership responsibilities, He called them to be servants. They were not to "lord it over" those who would follow them, but instead lay themselves down for the good of those they would lead. This "servant leadership" has been the focus of much discussion and many books in the centuries since.

What is servant leadership? Some describe it as the leadership you know with a strong grasp on humility: *Lead as you know to lead, but remember that Jesus is your leader, so keep your own sense of importance tightly in check.* That's a good idea in principle and the humility part is certainly important, but living it proves difficult to say the least. The temptation to dip one's toes in that prideful pool overcomes most of the servant leaders who take this "kinder, gentler" approach.

I think Jesus intended more than just a typical approach to leadership, minus the egotistical steroids.

True servant leadership is defined by that first word—*servant*. A servant is one who serves others, who gets his sense of direction from the needs he sees and can help meet, who finds his purpose in making the way smoother for others. In others words, serving is all about people. Jesus described the greatest form of love, "Greater love has no one than this: to lay down one's life for one's friends" (John 15:13). Jesus demonstrated that love Himself, illustrating for us a type of leader seldom seen. The road to His throne traveled through a cross. You don't see many leaders choosing that road.

> We're assigned to serve people with none of the more attractive goals of self-interest and acclaim.

Yet that's the path for us, too. Jesus said that if we wanted to follow Him, we would need to take up our own cross to do so (Matt. 16:24). We're not in the fast lane to comfort and applause. Instead, self-denial and sacrificial effort for the good of others is our road. We're assigned to serve people with none of the more attractive goals of self-interest and acclaim.

So how do you measure excellence in serving? Don't those served speak into that evaluation? Sure they do. The best servants are the ones who go the extra mile for people with no thought of reciprocation or even appreciation. Servants do what needs to be done because they're committed to the work assigned by the master.

They're committed to people.

This is what Jesus meant by servant leadership. Yes, His disciples would have roles in leading His church. They would make decisions and give direction to other servants, but only when their gaze turned toward people would they understand how to lead in Jesus' unique way.

You see, that's what motivates God to come toward us, too. Even in the Old Testament, we see God responding powerfully to the cries of His people. Whether with Moses and a generation of slaves or in the days of the judges when rival nations wreaked havoc on the daily lives of the Israelites, God responded by sending a leader who would conquer what had been conquering them. In Jesus, God provided His ultimate Savior because of His passion for us.

Jesus showed us that same passion when He looked out over Jerusalem and tearfully pleaded for them. Listen to His love despite their tragic history, a resilient love for us that fills God's heart yet today:

> Jerusalem, Jerusalem, you who kill the prophets and stone those sent to you, how often I have longed to gather your children together, as a hen gathers her chicks under her wings, and you were not willing. (Matt. 23:37)

Spirit-empowered disciples learn to see people like that. Why? Because God's heart has filled our hearts. When we see people in need, something breaks inside. So with compassion and a sense of divine purpose, we step into moments, even moments that are greater than our resources. We rely on God's provision, knowing His heart beats for those we have encountered.

Those who fixate simply on doing typically have their eyes focused elsewhere. They tend to imagine their responsibility is to fulfill needed tasks. So they attempt to master such assignments, becoming great preachers, remarkable teachers, or even leaders of large compassion-driven organizations. But over time their pursuit of excellence can get detached from the very people they hope to serve. Suddenly, people must take a back seat. The goal is to be the best, the greatest, or the person who can do what no one else has previously done. Jesus said this kind of leadership misses His mark.

When love for Christ and compassion for people drives our doing, something beautiful emerges—a sense of community or family that many are desperate to find. For most of us, family includes those people whom we know love us so much they would die for us. They give us the security we crave and the companionship so essential to healthy living. As we have seen, Jesus loved those no one else loved and welcomed them into God's family—an extraordinary concept.

That's what servant leadership does—it conveys value to every individual. When we serve, we send God's message of love in powerful ways. We prove that relationship with Him is possible because it can be seen in us. Through our commitment to people, the kingdom of God goes forward both in power and in love.

⁓

In the Spirit-empowered life, serving is a critical form of expression. But God doesn't just want our time or resources. He has a specific way for us to serve—one that helps us live in healthy relationship with Him. As we have seen, learning and doing often end in pride and exhaustion, but serving in God's pattern generates community and a true sense of God's family. It unleashes His remarkable power and love.

The Spirit-empowered disciple knows that serving is a key means of growth. Study and teaching alone cannot bring the life of God to us. Instead, we must engage our world through serving so we can learn fully all that God would teach us.

> Since we are following Christ and the Holy Spirit lays out the path before us, we can't become too attached to specific tasks or even the places where we do them.

Our serving must also be motivated by our love for Christ. Our desire for tasks or feelings of commitment to people will experience highs and lows, but our reasons to love Christ never wane. That love is the only enduring motivation for acts of service, and it's the only way our relationship with Him can grow amidst our doing. All other motives fail in times of difficulty, but our love for Christ becomes a bottomless resource when we consider how He has loved us.

Spirit-empowered serving also remembers who directs our steps. Since we are following Christ and the Holy Spirit lays out the path before us, we can't become too attached to specific tasks or even the places where we do them. God may choose to move us, to take one assignment from us in order to give us another, or to move us from hidden to visible places, and even back again. His ways are higher than ours (Isa. 55:8–9), and His purposes often elude us. So we live a life of faith—one where we trust the God who has called us and accept the places and work He knows will use us best.

Finally, the Spirit-empowered life calls for a commitment to people. The kingdom we serve has only one deserving King. He was given that exalted place by His own sacrificial commitment to others, and we know that the path to our own exaltation is paved with the humblest of stones. Jesus gave us His authority so we could continue His work and demonstrate His heart for others. That means a cross of self-denial for us, too. Someday we will share in His glory, but the road to such greatness travels through a willingness to put the needs of others ahead of our own.

In the end, this life of loving Christ and serving others provides our best fulfillment of His command: "Love the Lord your God with all your heart and with all your soul and with all your mind. . . . Love your neighbor as yourself" (Matt. 22:37, 39).

This is both our mission and the means by which it is fulfilled. And remarkably, such loving efforts to serve prove to be the most powerful way to change the world.

THINK ABOUT IT

1. Why should God's servants be more focused on people than on the tasks we provide for them?
2. How have other Christians affected you by their acts of serving?
3. What are some reasons why God might, at times, have you serve in smaller, less-visible ministries?

CHAPTER 29

Go: The Purpose for the Power

Our wonder at God's interest in relationship with us is only outdistanced by the stunning truth that He also wants to share His power with us. That's hard to imagine, but according to Jesus' own words, it's a part of His plan. *You shall receive power* . . .

Now most of us would be quick to admit that such an act could be risky. Given our tendency toward self-promotion, self-centeredness, and just about any other words that *self* can prefix, the idea of God's power in us seems a little edgy at best. Can He trust us to pursue His agenda and continue to funnel all attention and glory His direction? If He gives us His power, will we use it for our purposes or will we care for His kingdom?

Choice is God's most surprising gift, but one He continually extends to us. In the garden of Eden, Adam and Eve failed with their choice, opting to disregard God's clear instructions for a game plan drawn up by a snake. That hardly seems like a wise move, given the greatness God had already demonstrated. So there's your proof—the first guy and gal couldn't be counted on for a good decision. But we've been no better, each of us using our gift of choice to selfishly satisfy our own cravings, regardless of the better path God has offered. Had He given up on us . . . well, that would have made sense.

Instead, He not only died to open the door for relationship with us, but again put His eternal plan into our hands, choosing to make that plan dependent on our choice. And, the mode through which we would fulfill that plan would be His power—in us!

Jesus promised that power, and within a few days, God filled His disciples with the Holy Spirit, making them something they could never have been on their own. What would they do with the opportunity? Well, in their case, and in many since, better choices were made. In fact, the mission continues to us and to our day, even though some have failed along the way. God still puts His power into those who follow Him with the expectation that we have and will accept His mission to be His "witnesses" among our own people and beyond.

Still, there are those among the Spirit-filled community in today's church who have yet to commit to the mission. They have decided that Spirit-empowerment is for their own benefit, helping them live more focused Christian lives. Some wear their Spirit-filled status like a badge of achievement, as if experiencing the baptism in the Holy Spirit were without further purpose—an experience with nothing more than personal satisfaction at its root.

Yes, there are extraordinary potential benefits to what many call Spirit baptism. How could the powerful presence of the Holy Spirit within us not affect us in numerous ways? Shouldn't we more effectively say no to temptation? Shouldn't we more deeply understand God's love and more clearly know His guidance? Relationship with God is the centerpiece of our salvation, and the power of His Spirit would surely take that relationship to a whole new level.

But there's an even greater reason God places His power within us—*to fulfill the mission He has given us.* As we've already seen, we lack the capacity to fulfill God's Commission on our own. We simply don't have the ability to become what we aren't, to go where we've never been, and to do what can't be done in human strength. We've been given this extraordinary assignment and are absolutely dependent upon God if we are going to succeed in doing it.

> We've been given this extraordinary assignment and are absolutely dependent upon God if we are going to succeed in doing it.

So our want and our need depend on receiving Jesus' promise of the Spirit. How tragic it would be for us not to give ourselves to His purpose. Yet, that's what happens to some who have pursued and even received that promise.

The Spirit-empowered life is focused outward, not just in serving but in spreading the gospel message. As Jesus said, we are to be His "witnesses in Jerusalem, and in all Judea and Samaria, and to the ends of the earth" (Acts 1:8). To pursue the power God has offered for any other reason is to miss the whole point of His promise. God fills us with His power so we can do what He has designed us to do!

The early disciples understood this. There were many lessons to learn and issues to overcome as they moved forward. Their own ideas of who could have relationship with God had to be altered. In fact, it took three versions of the same vision for Simon Peter to accept that Gentiles could encounter God (Acts 10:9–16). As we saw, a deacon named Philip was among the first to head to Samaria, and did so before the apostles seemed ready to go there themselves. Still, even in their fledgling understanding of their mission and their limited grasp of the broader elements of their message, they knew they had a job to do—and the power they needed to do it.

Not long after Jesus' young church began impacting its home city, persecution broke out against it. The believers' unwillingness to worship the Roman emperor made them easy targets for extreme forms of cruelty. So they scattered, leaving Jerusalem in search of safer territory. Still, even as they went, they continued to preach Jesus' message of grace (Acts 8:4). They had been empowered to be witnesses wherever they went, and sharing His truth in the midst of their crisis proved their determination to get the job done. Pretty impressive, isn't it? One wonders why many of us in the Western world cower so easily to occasional criticism or ridicule when those who were given the same Holy Spirit proved willing to face so much more.

Our mission is outward, and our determination to live with such focus proves to be the critical ingredient to our strength and the continued health of our churches. When a congregation turns inward—a natural tendency over time—they lose their reason for being. Their gatherings end up as little more than exercises in their own preferences, doing what they like and expecting others to like it, too. These local churches begin living as though their leader is responsible to keep them happy, to care for their needs, and to somehow make their own selfish pursuits feel meaningful. Herein lies the basic reason so many congregations in the Western world have plateaued in their growth or have begun to decline. Outward focus is the

> Our mission is outward, and our determination to live with such focus proves to be the critical ingredient to our strength and the continued health of our churches.

essential ingredient to strength and health, just as it is essential for the life of the individual believer.

We've already seen how God established His church to be about "Him and them." Our love for Him and for others provides the fuel for His Commission and keeps our lives on track. Nowhere is that priority seen more clearly than in our efforts to connect with and reach out to those who have yet to engage relationship with Him.

While our collective effort as a local congregation is one way to live out our mandate, each of us must personally pursue our own contribution if we're going to live a life of power. It's not enough to applaud the efforts our "team" makes or celebrate what our church is doing. We must live the Spirit-empowered life ourselves.

That's why God chose to dwell within each of our hearts. Yes, it is accurate to say that the Spirit of God is in His church, but His days of living in buildings are long gone (Heb. 9:11). God doesn't give His Holy Spirit to a collective gathering or an organization. He places His Spirit in every believer with the clear intent that each of us will live a powerful journey.

But many try to follow Christ without experiencing His promise. They try learning and doing in an effort to please Him and participate in His kingdom, only to confront their own inadequacy and strength. Others may experience His power but fail to engage His mission. After a while, it seems that neither the power nor the passion it once brought are discernible in their lives. Few people are more dangerous to the mission of the local church than those who once possessed God's power but have allowed their own agendas to take over. These have the appearance of spiritual leaders and can even trace their experience back to a moment of empowering, but their failure to maintain an outward focus has drained them of all that such power might have accomplished.

Jesus promised that signs and wonders would follow those who obeyed His calling. He promised His presence and His power wherever His kingdom would be preached. But what promise is there for those who don't go?

It seems reasonable that there's a connection between the self-centeredness of many in Western Christianity and the powerlessness that seems equally evident. At the same time, in local settings both small and large, those who give themselves fully to God's worldwide mission find strength and blessing in large measure. And when our choice for that mission remains strong, we can expect God to continue to fuel our efforts. That's the reason for His promise.

And that's the nature and full expression of the Spirit-empowered life.

THINK ABOUT IT

1. In what way is inward focus an act of disobedience?
2. How might giving yourself to His mission actually be one of the best ways for you to grow in your relationship with Christ?

CHAPTER 30

Go: Risk

T hus far, we've said a lot about the possibilities, the increased capacity, and the amazing nature of the Spirit-empowered life, but there are reasons why the choice for such a life isn't unanimous. Only 120 followed Jesus all the way to the upper room, and many more have rejected than received that empowerment in the centuries since.

Sure, we could write off the choices others make as indicative of their self-centered preference for personal priorities, but that's not always the case. A life of sacrificial service doesn't connect with the desires of many, but there's more to the smaller crowd than that. Remember, Jesus told us we must take up our own cross if we want to follow Him, and what that means can be different for each of us.

Honestly, some don't seek God's promise because of fear. Giving God complete control over their future sounds good when His blessings are clearly flowing, but God's priorities often don't match the ones we would choose for ourselves. The fear of what God might want of them keeps many from that upper room experience.

Try putting yourself in the sandals of those early disciples shortly after Jesus' ascended. To that point, Jesus had provided everything they needed at every moment. Following Jesus meant exactly that—following. Jesus made decisions about where they would go, whose house they would dine at, and what they would do when the crowds chased them from across the lake. Following Jesus hadn't always been easy, but I'm guessing they would have been thrilled to have the certainty of His tangible presence back with them. In fact, some have suggested that their hopes of His quick return helped drive them to that upper room. If they were all truly of one mind that day, it was probably with thoughts like, *Jesus, we really miss You. Are You about to come back?* The horizon seemed unlimited, the potential destinations too many to count, and the directions of what to do less than clear. Did they have reasons to be fearful? You bet! But that didn't stop them.

Fear of the unknown cripples many would-be disciples. It seems much easier to settle for a comfortable wilderness life than to trust God for whatever battles might be ahead on the road to the Promised Land. How many times did Jesus say, "Be not afraid," to His disciples? The phrase kept coming up because their fears frequently mounted. Life today may be more technologically advanced with superior modes of transportation, but the path to the ends of the earth remains lined with reasons to fear.

If fear doesn't keep some at home, rejection might. Those who live Spirit-empowered lives have nearly always had to deal with rejection from those on other paths. One would think that those bringing good news would be welcomed enthusiastically (Isa. 52:7), but those who embrace the Spirit-empowered people aren't typically a majority either.

> Those who live Spirit-empowered lives have nearly always had to deal with rejection from those on other paths.

Many years ago, a prominent Spirit-empowered leader said, "You can't know Pentecost without knowing exile."[2] While his point specifically referenced the rejection many encountered in the early 1900s—locked out of their churches, ridiculed, falsely accused, and occasionally pelted with debris—his point remains valid, even in seemingly more open-minded settings. Those who believe God wants to empower His people today know the criticisms that others easily attach to their faith, the promises they believe, and the experiences they describe as God fulfills His promise. The power of the Holy Spirit repels as likely as it draws those who have yet to accept God's purposes for their lives.

Fear and rejection are two powerful motivators for the human psyche, but let's add a third—risk. What else would we call a life where we step into situations that are larger than our resources and try to achieve goals that are well beyond our capacity? In such moments, the ridicule and criticism often seem logical. To follow God's plan demands that everything be risked for a kingdom that only those of faith can see.

And God specializes in seeing in us what we can't see ourselves. He directs us down a path that overmatches us and wants us to trust that He will give us what we need for every moment. This is how the greatest stories of Spirit-empowered living always begin—with a challenge too great to be accomplished reasonably.

So many people reject the possibility of a life of more of God's power on these seemingly sensible grounds. But such risk of fear, rejection, and everything we possess is a key way the Spirit-empowered life is expressed. We must live on a ragged edge where the only certainty found in tomorrow is the presence of the One who bids us there.

Abraham knew the just would live by faith (Rom. 4). Moses was willing to lead his generation through any desert crisis as long as God would be with them (Ex. 33:15). David grabbed five rocks, confident not in his ability with his small weapon but in the God whom Goliath had mocked (1 Sam. 17:40). David only needed one stone for that giant, but the text does say that Goliath had four brothers—so David seems to have gathered all the ammo he might need.

The Spirit-empowered life requires boldness, but not a boldness drawn from self-confidence. There's no reason for any surety in ourselves. Instead, there must be a boldness to trust that God will fulfill His promise—the same God who gave the promised Holy Spirit to begin with. That's why people of all personalities step into Spirit-filled living. The brash must learn a different Source for their assuredness, and the meek must find a courage in their faith they never knew in themselves. This boldness doesn't come from what we bring to the table but what God brings. Our only contribution is the want and the need.

Sometimes that boldness must press through confusion. Simon Peter had a reasonably strong grasp of God's ways when he had a vision of a sheet filled with all types of unclean animals. At first, he refused the command to "get up, Peter . . . kill and eat," knowing that God had prohibited such things from his Jewish diet (Acts 10:13–14). But God was pushing him toward a new door, one that must have seemed confusing. As the vision instructed, Peter went with the Gentile men who had come for him, and later watched as the Holy Spirit fell on Gentiles in the same way Peter himself had experienced (vv. 44–46). When God is doing what we thought He'd never do . . . well, that's more than a bit confusing. But when we're led by God's Spirit, sometimes the answers we've been comfortable with don't fit the new questions we encounter.

We've become accustomed to Gentiles receiving salvation and the power of God's Spirit, but our issues draw their own lines. How willing are we to learn what we have not known? Will we require that God lead us only to what seems familiar or embrace only what we find tasteful? Can our hearts and minds be open to new mysteries, or must we recast God in our own image and require Him to do what we like or think acceptable? I'm guessing you know how the Spirit-empowered life might answer such questions.

This is a life that demands the willingness to grow, to lay aside any thought that we've got things figured out and that our systems or previous ideas have captured the sum total of God's work in the world. It's risky to put long-held ideas to the test. On some level, we remain confident that truth will prove itself and prevail, but it's not easy to remain open-minded, especially when we hear minds around us slamming shut.

Can we hunger to grow when that growth stretches us, demands more of us than we've ever given, and calls us to places beyond our proverbial comfort zone? This is the journey of the Spirit-empowered life, and it makes sense that things would be like this. What need would we have of God's Spirit if the challenges fit our paradigms or seemed evenly matched to our previous experiences? Why would we need to seek God's presence and help if what we confronted seemed comfortably within our current context? That the challenges ahead require more than we have to give seems to fit the whole idea of following God. The road would have to be pretty amazing to justify a need for His amazing power.

And that's an essential truth about the life God has for each of us. It's a life that requires Him. God's real vision for our lives has to be God-sized, doesn't it? If it weren't, then why would we have needed to wait for His power, as Acts 1:5 commands? The Spirit-empowered life can't be lived without the Spirit's power, so get ready for the ride of your life.

> The Spirit-empowered life can't be lived without the Spirit's power, so get ready for the ride of your life.

The apostle Paul called the Romans to offer themselves to God as "a living sacrifice" (Rom. 12:1). It seems clear from the context of his point that such a life wasn't reserved for spiritually elite forces or a special brand of Christ-follower. Some may think the Spirit-empowered life is just for a few highly dedicated Christians, but Paul described the choice to follow Christ fully as one that is our "true and proper worship." Jesus didn't die for just a few of us, but each person who embraces relationship with Him has the same set of reasons for pursuing His mission and His power.

There's a path of learning and experience for all who walk this Spirit-empowered road. There's much to encounter and plenty of room for faith to grow. God asks that we step into the moments before us, and He promises to give us what we need for every step. Those who think a single encounter with His Spirit will suffice for every future moment haven't read the book of Acts closely. Repeatedly the Holy Spirit showed up in the lives of the early disciples, sometimes speaking direction, other times giving needed boldness. When healings were needed, those experiences came as well. God repeatedly stepped into their lives to provide what they needed. They received so they could give—the same process by which God equips the Spirit-empowered today.

So yes, there's risk. There's fear and rejection to stare down and more than a few difficult barriers to cross. But by the power of God's Spirit, even the most unlikely circumstances can provide a place where God reveals His love and sufficiency through the lives of the Spirit-empowered.

THINK ABOUT IT

1. How have fear and rejection affected your efforts to pursue God's mission?
2. Why do you think God brings you to places of risk in your journey toward His purposes?

CHAPTER

31

Go: It May Mean Stay

Jesus said, "Go!" But what does that mean? Okay, *go* isn't the hardest word to define. When someone commands another to go, there's clearly a direction or even a destination in mind. And Jesus' directive fits that idea. He even mentioned target locations like Jerusalem, Judea, and beyond. Still, given the scope of that missional moment, one wonders if Jesus meant more than just mapped journeys. It seems likely He did.

"Go" can also mean to go *from here*. In other words, *stop what you're doing and do something else.* That's clearly the largest idea in Jesus' Commission. The days of sitting on hillsides and listening to His teaching were done. The assignment ahead was a new one where they would be the teachers. The sick would still be healed, but now it would be the disciples' hands extending that healing. From that point forward, "go" meant new direction, new activity, and a whole new world of engagement.

That's what it means for us as well. Once we are in relationship with Jesus, His heart begins to grow inside of us. As He instructs, we wait for His promise of power, and when it comes, everything changes. The mission is now in our hands. The destinies are wider and more varied than we imagine. He opens doors, sends us forward, and we go, ready to do what He will equip us to do. Go means *go and do what you've never done before!*

Inherent in His command is the idea to *get off the bench, test out those legs, and put into practice what He has been preparing you to do.* The directive is clearly outward. To this point, we may have been watching and even occasionally helping as He ministered to the needs around us. But otherwise, our focus has been inward—learning all we can and experiencing the changes He has brought to our lives. He has been ministering to our needs and freeing us from things that would hold us back. He's been giving us His heart and teaching us His ways, all with a launch day in mind—one we will know has come when He fulfills His promise of power.

Now, Jesus will keep on ministering to us, even as we engage the "go" command He has for our lives. There will always be places for us to grow, to be stretched by His purpose, to encounter changes in our understandings, and to enlarge our faith.

As we have seen, there was still much for the disciples to learn. There were life lessons that only experiences on the road ahead could teach. But the command to go meant the mission had begun. Focus had shifted to an outward purpose, for they had been commissioned and empowered with the kingdom of God.

> There will always be places for us to grow, to be stretched by His purpose, to encounter changes in our understandings, and to enlarge our faith.

Has your focus shifted as well? Notice that Jesus gave the Commission before the promise of the Holy Spirit was fulfilled. That's why the "wait" in Acts 1:5 was necessary. Jesus' sending words rang in their ears for several days, maybe even a few weeks, before the events of Acts 2 unfolded. Why? Because the commission stirs our hunger. Its challenge, coupled with the heart growing inside us, makes our pursuit of His promise even more passionate. By the time the day of Pentecost came, they were all united in a single desire—*God, give us the promise of the Holy Spirit!*

Jesus told us something quite interesting about the gift-giving ways of His Father:

> If you then, though you are evil, know how to give good
> gifts to your children, how much more will your Father
> in heaven give the Holy Spirit to those who ask him!
> (Luke 11:13)

We ask because the desire to fulfill His purpose is growing within us. We ask because we're desperate to sacrifice our lives as a thank-you card for all God has given us. We ask because we love Him and want to see His kingdom come to the lives of others. So, in spite of the unknown and the risk we sense on the horizon, we ask for the Holy Spirit to send us forward with His power. It's our hunger for the Commission that drives our pursuit of God's Spirit. We want to go!

And when that moment comes, there are two extremes on the destination continuum—Jerusalem and the ends of the earth (Acts 1:8). As we've seen, these are more than points on a map. They represent two different mentalities that must merge in the heart of every Spirit-empowered disciple.

First, let's consider Jerusalem. This capital city was the nexus point of the gospel and the birthplace of the church. For the disciples, Jerusalem represented everything that was familiar. They knew its streets, its customs, and its people. And its people knew them. On the day of Pentecost, even the puzzled crowd outside recognized them and the region of their birth. Jerusalem held few mysteries for the disciples, and the new direction of their lives seemed difficult for their longtime friends to grasp.

For some, "Go!" means *stay* geographically. Theirs is an assignment amidst the familiar—no new languages or customs to master, but still much to overcome. You see, while the familiar setting of home turf offers distinct advantages, the available traps are just as familiar. Living a new life before friends absolutely requires God's power. How else can we be what we've never been in the places where we've been something else?

And certainly, those who have known us struggle to see us in that new light. Even Jesus found things difficult among the people of His hometown. After encountering their criticism and lack of faith, He commented that "a prophet is not without honor except in his own town and in his own home" (Matt. 13:57). And we know that His brothers (half-brothers, actually) found it difficult to imagine their older sibling as the Son of God. I have a younger sister, and I can see how that would be hard (especially for her).

To those who head toward uttermost places, life in Jerusalem may seem easy, but it's not. Going to those we know brings equal or even greater risk of rejection. Even the most Spirit-empowered life often has to be lived consistently over lengthy periods of time before those nearby will acknowledge its difference. What we speak must be in demonstration. Words are seldom enough in Jerusalem. The life proclaimed must be on display.

Unfortunately, many who claim to be filled with God's Spirit seem to prefer living their powerful lives together on Sundays while failing to match that fervor throughout their week. These "church-house Pentecostals" give great attention to the work and the gifts of the Spirit in the safety of their gatherings, but then seem to disconnect with their Source of power during the week. Such a pattern is difficult for others to interpret—especially those closest to them (spouses, children, coworkers). The usual conclusion is hypocrisy, one that keeps those who see it from believing such a life could have anything to offer them.

The Spirit-empowered life certainly has much to express through times of worship with fellow believers, but this life finds its greatest demonstration as light amidst darkness. The marketplace is where the power is most needed. And in Jerusalem, the marketplace must be the focus. When people see how our lives shine as we move in the real places of our familiar city, they begin to see a difference in us that proves attractive.

Words matter in Jerusalem as well. Once people have seen something new in us, they need clear understanding of how we have changed. It's the presence of Christ in us that has brought a new day. Words become necessary when they perceive the light so they can know that such light is within their grasp as well. Those who never explain the hope

> Those who never explain the hope that is within them seldom get to celebrate the new birth of those they love.

that is within them seldom get to celebrate the new birth of those they love.

In the end, Jerusalem is watching. Though reluctant to believe, those who dwell in our Jerusalem need hope, too. They are just as trapped in failing destinations as those we find across the globe. They are just as hungry and just as desperate to find something worth living and dying for. To abandon them by living boring lives is especially cold-hearted. This is our first mission field—the one most easily within reach.

Distant places (the subject of our next chapter) matter, too. But in many local churches, the focus has centered on the far away to the exclusion of all other fields. Christians have been compelled to give rather than to live in a way that reflects their worldwide assignment. Without question, giving matters much to harvest fields everywhere, but our wallets can't replace our feet when it comes to pursuing God's purposes for our lives.

The Spirit-empowered among us who are called to stay find their hearts breaking for those they know and the way of life they have grown to love. They long to bring hope to the high school hallways they've walked and the grocery store aisles they've shopped. They see the familiar faces of their workplaces in a whole new light and long to rescue friends from the paths they once walked themselves.

The Spirit-empowered who stay know they've been called to Jerusalem and look for opportunities to bring God's power into the worlds they know.

While many will engage the distant roads of the earth's outer edges, most who engage the Spirit-empowered life have found their mission field at home.

THINK ABOUT IT

1. Do you find it difficult to discuss your relationship with God among family or friends?
2. What steps can you take to demonstrate more effectively that relationship in your Jerusalem?

C H A P T E R
32

Go: Finding the Edges

While we have already considered a number of ways that a Spirit-empowered life is expressed, none is more stunning and remarkable than the worldwide spread of such people in the name of the Savior. The Spirit-empowered who have been called to go have been filled with the power of the Holy Spirit and have distinguished themselves by their determination to take the gospel to places it may have never been.

The whole idea of "the ends of the earth" sounds compelling, doesn't it? It conveys the idea of an edge, an outer rim, or the point farthest from where one now stands. Those with such a spirit embrace the unknown and discover realities to relay back to those closer to the familiar. They explore and encounter what few have found and often find God's power demonstrated most extraordinarily. In fact, there almost seems to be an inverse relationship between the numbers of miracles performed and the number of people who have heard Jesus' name. For those who haven't heard, God often brings evidence of His love and power in abundance.

Indeed, the "ends" implies distant places. When Jesus first gave His words of Commission, the disciples knew little of what lay beyond the land of Israel. The Roman empire stretched some distance in nearly all directions and was surprisingly accessible through roads and waterways, but beyond was a mystery and few could imagine such a horizon. Still they took His message and His command to make disciples, and several traveled well past their boyhood homes. There's even some evidence of the original Twelve preaching among peoples beyond the areas controlled by Rome. And church history tells us that each of them paid an amazing price amidst the persecution they encountered.

Today the world is a lot smaller. Advances in transportation have made travel to just about anywhere on the planet a legitimate possibility. Yet, the Spirit-empowered don't limit themselves to places easily found on maps. Instead, they seek "the ends" with the gospel, deeming even the most remote natives worthy of their lives. For the Spirit-empowered who push against such boundaries, others simply watch in awe and shout praise to God.

But the ends of the earth can mean more than geographical locales. Even in lands where the message of Christ has flourished, there are people who have never heard about Christ and circumstances that have never been addressed. Even in neighborhoods where churches dot the street corners, there are pockets of people who get overlooked. It takes an "ends of the earth" mentality to begin ministering among a forgotten people in your own city. For some, it's the homeless or the harmed that grabs their attention. For others, those who are trapped in sinful choices form a target audience. Still others find their purpose where only new ideas can get the job done. Ends means edges, and God continually raises up His Spirit-empowered disciples to push that edge until it encompasses every individual.

> God often demonstrates His unlimited creativity in the kind of work He establishes to reveal His love and purpose.

Ends can also mean new approaches. God often demonstrates His unlimited creativity in the kind of work He establishes to reveal His love and purpose. Where once a single idea of the church might have been common throughout the Western world, today ministry concepts offer a variety of avenues for the gospel to travel to uttermost people. Those living Spirit-empowered lives continue to force out the edges.

Shouldn't those led by the Holy Spirit be on the leading edge of creativity? Shouldn't the best and brightest ideas come from those who are led by the presence of God within? When the apostles launched their mission, local religious leaders couldn't believe what these unschooled men were doing. In fact, one of their leaders calmed those who opposed them by saying,

> Leave these men alone! Let them go! For if their purpose or activity is of human origin, it will fail. But if it is from God, you will not be able to stop these men; you will only find yourselves fighting against God. (Acts 5:38–39)

It's hard to imagine wanting to be found in opposition to what God's Spirit is directing.

Perhaps the most remarkable part of considering what happens on the uttermost edge is the kind of people who live Spirit-empowered lives there. You would think those places would be venues for mavericks, for those who have made their name with risk or with little attachment to comfortable places. But many who trust God for such extraordinary exploits seem surprisingly common. They're not supermen or folks who missed out on the "home" chromosome the rest of us carry. They have families and care deeply for the grandchildren they rarely see. Like many whose stories dot the pages of Scripture, there's nothing unusual about them that explains their amazing path.

That's the surprising truth about Spirit-empowered people. They usually look just like the rest of us. The difference is in the plan of the One who possesses them and in their willingness to believe Him for the seemingly impossible.

Have you ever stopped to consider that the comfortable place you call home—the spot many Christ-followers are reluctant to leave—was an end of the earth place to the original disciples? Yet Spirit-empowered people faithfully followed God's unique direction and brought the chance for relationship with Him to our shores one day. What many might have once labeled a Christian nation wasn't even on the early church's map, and perhaps future places where the gospel might thrive could look a bit desolate on the faith meter at the moment.

That's why the end-time glimpses we get of God's throne room include people "from every nation, tribe, people and language" (Rev. 7:9). He is "not wanting anyone to perish, but everyone to come to repentance" (2 Peter 3:9). It's Spirit-empowered people who drive that mission and help Him fulfill His passion for those in distant places.

> When God is on our side, can any situation be truly impossible?

Spirit-empowered people find a way. We don't let reason and resources hinder our vision. After all, when God is on our side, can any situation be truly impossible?

There's no stronger indicator of a Spirit-empowered life than one's commitment to "go" as Jesus commanded. God gives His power for this reason; therefore, it naturally follows that our pursuit of His mission would result. And that outward focus keeps the power of the Spirit alive in us. He promised to punctuate our efforts with sign and wonders (Mark 16:17), but we must go among those where miraculous signs are needed.

Jesus told His disciples that our love for Him was best expressed by obedience to His commands (John 14:23). Making disciples of all nations is the centerpiece of those commands and the work that brings all other acts of obedience into reason. To experience God's power through our lives, we must obey what God has *already* spoken to us clearly.

∞

As we have seen, the Spirit-empowered life presents many moments of risk. While one could argue that depending on God would actually be the least risky way to live, still we find its uncertainty as challenging. Our comfort level is generally higher when we're convinced we already have what we need to do what we've already determined to accomplish. Leaving both the direction and the resources in God's hands opens us to a much wider array of possibilities.

There is risk whether we live our calling in our Jerusalem or in the uttermost places. The familiar world of home has many challenges, such as overcoming our past behaviors or living in a way that proves the changes Jesus has made. We can't neglect Jerusalem and run toward the more exciting fringes; we must be committed to those already within our circle of love.

But the Commission also compels us farther. The challenge of end-of-the-earth horizons offers plenty of evidence that God is with us. And what a remarkable moment it can be when we are able to present the fruit of such extraordinary journeys to the God who has called us.

As with serving, our efforts to go provide numerous moments that grow us more and more into the image of Christ. The more our dependence on God is exercised, the more freedom we give His Spirit to work within us. Our going will change the world, but it will also change us along the way.

When Jesus begged us to "lift up our eyes," He was showing us the path to life—real life. Only through our willingness to respond to His call can we find purpose, power, and the means by which both are kept alive within us. Simply put, if we don't go, we won't grow!

As we have said, there is no greater proof of the Spirit-empowered life than whether or not we've connected our feet to His mission. While signs and unique experiences mark the moment when God's Spirit fills us, it's our presence on the road ahead that truly reveals His Spirit within us. And since that first day of Pentecost when God's Spirit was poured out in great power,

He has continued to launch people into His kingdom mission, armed with truth, and eyes fixed on unlikely destinations. God is at war with hopelessness, brokenness, and the ravages of sin, and Spirit-empowered people are His army. And we are destined to make an amazing difference!

THINK ABOUT IT

1. What are some of the "ends-of-the-earth" efforts you are familiar with? What have you noticed about the people who serve there?
2. How might God be speaking to you about obeying His command to "go"?

CHAPTER 33

Worship: Expressing the Spirit

In the New Testament, Spirit-empowered people were best known for their extraordinary pursuit of mission. Today, however, it seems these Spirit-driven saints are sometimes better known for the uniqueness of their worship. In truth, the two should never be separated.

Since the beginnings of the modern Pentecostal movement (circa 1900), the worship gatherings of these Spirit-driven people have garnered much attention. Their meetings offered extended revivalist campaigns, reports of unusual manifestations, and celebratory praise often heard for blocks. Some would attend just to watch the odd events and then be caught up in the moments themselves, many finding their lives significantly changed.

More recently, such gatherings have waned a bit, save for those who remember them well and their hope to revive such experiences for a new generation. Today, most connect the idea of Spirit-filled worship with contemporary music, raised hands, and a priority on audience participation. In fact, some churches engage these worship practices in spite of their doctrinal resistance to experiences like the baptism in the Holy Spirit, divine healing, or the pursuit of various spiritual gifts. They like their idea of Spirit-filled worship but maintain a reluctance to allow many of the freedoms more common among those who are Spirit-empowered.

Do any of these expressions reflect true Spirit-empowered worship? What should one expect in the corporate gatherings of the Spirit-empowered? In fact, what might a Spirit-empowered disciple anticipate from their own life of worshipping God? These are important questions to be explored, both for fully demonstrating the Spirit-empowered life and for overcoming the resistance many feel when they encounter such things. It is here—at the matter of Spirit-empowered worship—that some allow their own hesitancy and uncertainty to build a wall between them and receiving God's promise.

First, true Spirit-empowered worship could never be about forms or specific methods. As we have said repeatedly, the Spirit-empowered life begins and is founded on a close relationship with God. No specific practice or even spiritual gift can substitute for the intimacy that characterizes Spirit-empowered worship. Those who identify a certain style of music or physical expression (like hand-raising) as uniquely Pentecostal or Spirit-empowered have yet to understand what those terms really mean.

> No specific practice or even spiritual gift can substitute for the intimacy that characterizes Spirit-empowered worship.

Throughout its history and into whatever future the church has this side of Christ's return, Jesus' disciples have expressed themselves to Him in adoration and thanksgiving through a wide variety of ways. These varied means of worship tend to be more connected to their own culture than any single, one-size-fits-all approach that might be maintained through the ages. The Spirit-empowered do seem more open than most to integrating worship practices that are relevant to their culture, likely because they prioritize true relationship with God. In such a relationship, one would expect to express himself to God in ways that truly reflect his own heart. The language or style of either former or future generations hardly helps "me be me" when I come to God in worship. To act as others have acted in the past might connect me to them in a nostalgic sense, but those approaches don't connect me to God any more effectively than what I might express from my own heart. The so-called "worship wars" are clearly more about us than about God.

Spirit-empowered worship isn't connected to any specific musical style or physical expression, but it's not specifically connected to any manifestation or specific gift either. Even as I write that sentence, I can sense some resistance from a few Acts 2 friends, but it's the openness to such things that characterizes the Spirit-empowered, not just the insistence that certain gifts be in evidence. While gifts and manifestations are often indicators that God's Spirit is at work in such moments, especially when those experiences can be understood and interpreted through Scripture, it's not the gift alone that is desired or even the primary goal. The presence and work of the Holy Spirit in our lives takes the pre-eminent spot.

The apostle Paul taught us that the gifts of the Holy Spirit are an important means by which God gives us what He knows we need (1 Cor. 12:7–11). Remember that for Spirit-empowered disciples, everything flows from experiencing God and His truth. We give what we have received, so frankly, there can be no giving without that receiving. To reject the possibility of receiving spiritual gifts would seem to significantly trim such equipping and leave us with little more than our own learning and doing. Yes, God can empower our efforts to learn and do, but again, how will He do that if we reject or de-emphasize some of His primary delivery methods?

Certainly, gifts and manifestations must be governed by God's revealed truth, but their occasional misuse doesn't invalidate their importance. These moments of missteps or excesses should never justify rejecting the whole. Paul brought needed correction to his friends at Corinth but applauded their sincere pursuit of such things. With the same passion, the Spirit-empowered hunger for every way God desires to touch their lives, even as they learn to express those moments in the ways God has prescribed.

> The Spirit-empowered hunger for every way God desires to touch their lives, even as they learn to express those moments in the ways God has prescribed.

Still, even with the priority placed on these experiences of God's equipping, gifts and expressions of worship do not characterize Spirit-empowered worship themselves. Instead, the Spirit-empowered know that expressions of worship seek God Himself. We long for every moment in His presence, knowing such occasions are transforming and give us opportunity to communicate our deep love for the One who has opened His door to us. Worship for the Spirit-empowered, then, is about connecting with God *on His terms and not on our own*. We come to God ready for Him to take the conversational lead and bring whatever He knows we need for the path ahead. We don't build fences around specific experiences or keep God from using them. Ours is a fully open pursuit where the One pursued is fully in charge.

You see, the Spirit-empowered know that worship is first and foremost a desire to honor God. His worthiness is unquestioned, and His holiness is to be admired and celebrated. God is not worshipped for what He might do, but for who He is and what He has already done. Even if He were never to lift His powerful finger on our behalf again, the Spirit-empowered know that God is worthy of an effort of worship that would exceed the remainder of our lives.

In the midst of that worship, God changes us. He equips us for the work He has for us, fulfills His promise of the Holy Spirit within us, and helps us understand the road ahead through eyes that are lifted to see what He sees. Times of worship aren't simply for generating good feelings or thinking we are spiritual. The purpose is to experience more of the One who has loved us extraordinarily.

The Spirit-empowered engage acts of worship with one goal in mind—to meet with God. We speak of God as One we can know and we talk of His presence surrounding us and filling us. We lay aside the routine of daily life for the hope that God will break in and bring the extraordinary.

One such expression that is unique to the Spirit-empowered is what many refer to as "praying in the Spirit." Through times of praying in unknown tongues, these followers of Christ express their hearts to God in ways that may seem puzzling to others. But this type of praying was clearly important to the apostles. Paul claimed to pray in the Spirit as much or more than anyone (1 Cor. 14:18), while Jude encouraged his readers to build themselves up in this way (Jude v. 20).

Why is there power in such prayer? Paul tells us that when we pray in this manner, the Holy Spirit Himself is praying with and through us (Rom. 8:26–27), even helping us pray when we aren't sure how to pray as we should.

Now, that same apostle helps us understand that the use of such prayer in a corporate setting requires someone to express the companion gift of interpretation. That way others can understand, thus eliminating any chaos or confusion. Through that same gift we may, at times, also understand the Spirit's prayer in our private moments, but in the Spirit-empowered disciple's daily times of praying in the Spirit such clarification isn't required. So Paul gladly states, "I will pray with my spirit, but I will also pray with my understanding; I will sing with my spirit, but I will also sing with my understanding" (1 Cor. 14:15).

The Spirit-empowered disciple says, "Me, too!" But the passion for such prayer isn't to create a mystical experience or feeling of spiritual superiority. Instead, the Spirit-empowered hunger for the strength and encouragement that comes from such intimacy with God. As Jesus pointed out, those who seek their friends' attention or applause for their public pursuit of God won't receive much attention from the One they claim to pursue (Matt. 6:1).

Worship for the Spirit-empowered offers the hope of deepening relationship and life-altering experiences in God's presence. In fact, most of these disciples will say that worship hasn't begun *until I have met with God.* For that reason, some will spend hours worshipping God, waiting for Him to engage them.

Now, we must never focus too heavily on any individual experience, lest the experience itself become the goal. When people focus too heavily on specific experiences, God becomes little more than the "delivery boy" to their desires. They are not truly worshipping Him but waiting for Him to provide whatever they might have set their hearts on. In fact, while some may have found ways to such desired experiences, without the presence of God intimately connected to their moments the proof of His real power is often lacking.

Because many judge Spirit-filled worship by its outward and occasionally unusual demonstrations, it may be accurate to say that one must be truly Spirit-empowered to know the truth about such expressions. To the Spirit-empowered, the outward is always secondary to the intimacy with God pursued within. That's where the relationship occurs and the true life-changing impact takes place. As we hunger for God, rather than what He can do for us, He lets us come close to Him, to know Him more, and to hear His passion more clearly (James 4:8).

It is this desire that governs Spirit-empowered worship and offers the best explanation as to why we fully engage such moments wholeheartedly. We can't imagine standing idle or disinterested when calling out to God. We can't fathom entering God's presence unprepared or with little enthusiasm for the possibilities of such encounters. We come to meet with God, whether in a group setting or in private moments.

So what should one expect in corporate gatherings of the Spirit-empowered? There will be a passion for God and a deep desire to meet with Him in whatever way He might desire. That's the nature of the freedom in worship we often speak about—not a freedom to do what we want to express ourselves, but a freedom where God can do as He wants with us and can speak into our lives in both familiar and unique ways.

THINK ABOUT IT

1. How do you express your wholehearted openness to God through worship?
2. What boundaries have you placed on God for such moments? Do you think God may want more freedom in your life than you've been willing to give Him?

CHAPTER
34

Worship: Celebrating the God We Know

Something happens when we enter the presence of God. There's an undoing, an exposure of our hearts that reveals every weakness and flaw. What else could possibly result from a perfect God's encounter with imperfect beings like us?

But many have different expectations when they participate in worship. They're searching for good feelings, for an elevated sense of worth, or some worship experience that "ministers to them." They emerge from church services like they leave department stores, deciding if they got what they wanted or if they should try a different "store" next time. *"What I got out of it"* is the focus, an evident sign that consumerism has infiltrated the local church.

Shouldn't the One worshipped be the primary recipient of worship? Imagine a worshipper in the Old Testament temple wondering which Levite might kill the animal he brought in the most pleasing way. *Personally, I prefer the way that guy killed my bull last year, you know, less bloody and he had such a serene look on his face (the bull, I mean).* Really? When we're determined to be the primary recipient in a worship setting, we likely look just as foolish.

In those temple days, they called the moment of worship a "sacrifice," and it wasn't simply because the animal gave its life. Sacrifice meant humbly acknowledging sin and looking to God for mercy. It meant pouring oneself out before Him, even though the blood of the slaughtered animal symbolized that pouring. Worship cost the worshipper something.

I suspect the idea of worship hasn't really changed much. Of course, Jesus' sacrifice put an end to zoo sounds at church, but the need for humble expressions and sacrificial attitudes remains. God has shown Himself a unique blend of complete holiness and unconditional love, uncompromising righteousness and tender mercy, and both sides of that coin are revealed in true acts of worship.

Something important, powerful, and difficult happens when we worship God. To be in His presence means we encounter the God whose nearness overwhelmed those whose similar moments are recorded in the Bible. Ask Moses about being near to God when he carefully removed his sandals before a bush God had touched (Ex. 3:5–6). Ask Elijah about the fire and earthquake that shook him from his depression (1 Kings 19:11–13). God wasn't even in those powerful displays given to Elijah—they were His entourage—but God Himself came near in just a whisper. Ask John, the young man who had walked with Jesus every day. As an old man, he entered Christ's presence and fell down like a dead man (Rev. 1:17–18). Responses may vary, but being overwhelmed by the awesomeness of God is clearly a common thread.

> Something important, powerful, and difficult happens when we worship God.

Spirit-empowered disciples aren't casual about God's holiness. They know there's something immense and even fearful about drawing close to Him. Yes, Jesus' sacrifice has opened that door, but stepping in is still an intense experience. That's why everything about relationship with God begins with repentance. Jesus said we must discover a poverty of spirit (Matt. 5:3). We can't get close to God without the brightness of His glory revealing every speck of darkness in our hearts.

Isaiah's encounter with God shows this clearly. Read how this remarkable prophet began his journey with God:

> In the year that King Uzziah died, I saw the Lord, high and exalted, seated on a throne; and the train of his robe filled the temple. Above him were seraphim, each with six wings: With two wings they covered their faces, with two they covered their feet, and with two they were flying. And they were calling to one another: "Holy, holy, holy is the LORD Almighty; the whole earth is full of his glory." At the sound of their voices the doorposts and thresholds shook and the temple was filled with smoke.
>
> "Woe to me!" I cried. "I am ruined! For I am a man of unclean lips, and I live among a people of unclean lips, and my eyes have seen the King, the LORD Almighty."

> Then one of the seraphim flew to me with a live coal in his hand, which he had taken with tongs from the altar. With it he touched my mouth and said, "See, this has touched your lips; your guilt is taken away and your sin atoned for."
>
> Then I heard the voice of the Lord saying, "Whom shall I send? And who will go for us?"
>
> And I said, "Here am I. Send me!" (Isa. 6:1–8)

You can't miss the amazing sight that confronted Isaiah in this remarkable scene. Flying seraphim, smoke, shaking doorposts, and an eerie cry proclaiming God's holiness. There's a lot of "wow factor" in his effort to describe this place.

But it's Isaiah's reaction that demands our attention. We can't really picture what he saw, but we can grasp what he felt—and it wasn't pleasant at first. In that moment where the white-hot reality of God's immense holiness was on display, Isaiah could see the blackness that filled his own life. No wonder the Jews had long believed that no one could see God and live (Judg. 13:22). Isaiah was convinced he was a goner.

By comparison, I think Isaiah would compare favorably to most of us. If God graded on a curve, this upstanding, well-educated prophet would place higher in the grade book than we would, so I'm guessing a similar moment for us wouldn't prove more pleasant. To stand in God's presence would make anyone desperate for a hiding place.

> To stand in God's presence would make anyone desperate for a hiding place.

But God has a plan. For Isaiah, a coal from His altar burned away the prophet's sin. For us, that burning coal is Jesus Himself. Because of His sacrifice, we too are made new and can survive and even thrive in that remarkable place.

The point is that our encounter with God begins with brokenness. We don't dance a celebratory jig in God's throne room or rejoice at the good fortune of our access without first having relationship restored. The children of Israel begged Moses to send God away as they were overwhelmed by His nearness. Their sense of inadequacy was more than they could bear.

But Moses went up the mountain toward God. He had no reason for greater confidence in his own holiness, but he knew God had called him there and he wanted every piece of God's plan for his life. Moses, like Isaiah, was ready to serve God wholeheartedly. His first experiences in God's presence ultimately made him want to be there more and more.

Spirit-empowered disciples are like that. We know of our own unworthiness, and that God is every bit as majestic and awesome as the Bible attempts to describe. We've felt our own undoing in His presence, yet something makes us hunger to be there again and again.

Something makes us want to lay aside our own life plans when we hear what Isaiah heard. There, where self-focus had reigned for a moment, Isaiah overheard more than just the seraphim's cries of God's holiness. He heard a cry from the One on the throne, and that cry sounded different. There was no question in the seraphim's voice, for God's holiness is an established fact. But God's voice faltered, as if somehow the self-existent and all-sufficient One required something He did not possess—a choice He had given someone else the power to make.

Who will go for us?

Now there are more than a few occasions in the Bible where I wouldn't necessarily want to be present. There are even such moments in this story. But what comes next defines the heart's desire of every Spirit-empowered disciple. We long to answer God's question just as Isaiah did.

Here am I, send me!

I added the exclamation point, but I'm pretty sure Isaiah's volume level would have demanded one. To raise one's hand to God's mission may well be the greatest expression possible for humanity. This is the result of entering God's presence, the true purpose of His self-revelation.

This is what worship looks like in the life of the Spirit-empowered. There is a reflection and awe of God's real presence, and a keen awareness of our own weakened ability to respond. There is the relief of God's mercy and cleansing, and we can't get out of that place without hearing the heart of the One worshipped. Spirit-empowered disciples long to meet God, and we emerge from such encounters with deepened resolve and determined dependence on the One who has called us. No wonder such worship proves life-changing.

Such worship drives disciples back to the familiar place of want and need. The longing and hunger to be in God's immense presence underscores our own inadequacy and makes pursuing Him and His power that much more essential. To be with God is to need Him, to further distance ourselves from any reason for pride, and to hear His heart again and again.

Those who live Spirit-empowered lives know that worshipping God doesn't pump us up but propels us out into the arena where He longs to be most visible. In humble obedience, we sacrifice ourselves for His great purpose and know that every step we take is about Him and not about us. For how could true worship of God ever be about us?

THINK ABOUT IT

1. How have you experienced a sense of unworthiness as you worship God?
2. In such moments, have you heard God's heart for those around you?

CHAPTER 35

Worship: All Week Long

There's more to worship than singing. Somehow, worship seems to have been equated with a Sunday morning experience, but those who live Spirit-empowered lives know it's much more. In fact, true worship encompasses and centers on the way life is lived the other six days of the week. That's not to devalue Sunday morning worship times or to neglect the gathering of fellow believers in any way. But the idea that worship is reserved for one day each week completely misunderstands relationship with God. It virtually guarantees that a Spirit-empowered life won't be found.

Some Christ-followers think that Sundays provide the "fuel" they need to live a righteous life the rest of the week. The encouragement and instruction provided by the local church on Sunday generates the needed energy to keep them "charged up" to make good choices Monday through Saturday. If they miss too many Sundays they become weak and are an easy target for temptation's advances.

Now, as we certainly want to affirm, Sundays do matter. They are intended for encouragement and instruction. The gatherings of the saints can provide much in our pursuit of Spirit-empowered living, but they are not the "fueling" station that helps us endure. Instead, living every day as an act of worship by giving ourselves to Christ's mission is what provides the enduring fuel.

When Jesus sat by the well in Samaria waiting for His disciples to return with lunch, we know He had an amazing missional conversation with a woman. When the disciples returned with food, Jesus turned it down. He may have gone ahead and eaten with them, but He added, "My food . . . is to do the will of him who sent me" (John 4:34).

Now we've already discussed this story from the disciples' viewpoint, but Jesus' focus is important for the Spirit-empowered. He was clearly saying

He found His strength, even His nourishment, from doing what the Father had given Him to do. And that's what the Spirit-empowered have discovered as well. We know that our "fuel" is to serve God's purpose. We don't require weekly "recharging" because every day is an opportunity to live in the increasing power of God's Spirit. Sundays provide fellowship, instruction, and the celebration of life together, but Mondays should be just as potent, if not more so.

> Sundays provide fellowship, instruction, and the celebration of life together, but Mondays should be just as potent, if not more so.

In fact, the Spirit-empowered quickly discover that the Pentecostal experience loses its power when worship is divorced from daily life. God didn't give us that power for ourselves or to enhance our worship experiences. He empowered us to be witnesses wherever life might take us.

Honestly, it can seem easier to keep Sunday in its well-framed compartment. To take the instruction and encouragement we receive among those of like belief out there where people don't believe can be a bit difficult, if not frightening. Having "work life" and "family life" in their self-contained packages means we can focus on one thing at a time. So if we limit our effort for God to a specific time each week, that makes our to-do lists easier to track—daytimes for work, evenings for family, Saturdays for home projects, and Sundays for God (with two weeks off each year for vacation). That sounds like a manageable plan.

Except that God wants it all.

His plan is to magnify and multiply our relationship with Him in a way that changes everything about our daytimes, evenings, Saturdays, and even Sundays. (He can maximize our vacations, too!) No, it's not church all day every day; it's life—the way it was meant to be lived!

So let's consider what that looks like.

First, the Spirit-empowered take charge of their own growth. We don't limit our instruction in God's Word to the pastor's weekly insights. We dive into God's Word on our own, often daily, as we seek to better understand the God we love and the life He's designed for us to live. The Bible plays a central role in our worship for it provides guidance for life—and to the Spirit-empowered, worship is life.

We pray daily, too, actually even more often than that. Paul's suggestion to "pray continually" (1 Thess. 5:17) seems odd and even overwhelming to some believers, but that's usually because they view prayer as a formal event. They see the dignified, organized, and sometimes verbose prayers of Sunday morning church services and think, *How could I do that all the time? I'd never get anything done!*

For the Spirit-empowered, prayer is a fluid and ongoing conversation with God. We live with an awareness of His presence every day and know He is with us—close enough to hear our whispered thankfulness and requests for help. We see suffering and talk to God about it. We encounter a need and immediately ask God for help to meet it. We don't stop life to pray; we move horizontally while communicating vertically. That's how Spirit-empowered disciples try to live.

> For the Spirit-empowered, prayer is a fluid and ongoing conversation with God.

It makes sense. When we know God is our Source, and we readily admit we need Him and His power to be what He has called us to be, we want to communicate with Him at every opportunity. The more we pray, the less we rely on our own strength or lay awake at night mulling over the challenges ahead. If relationship requires communication—and it does—then our most important relationship demands the most communication. Prayer, both the formal and the more ongoing kind, is a key means for that to occur.

Of course, there are two sides to communication, so listening to God's voice becomes the steady habit of the Spirit-empowered. Jesus said that His "sheep listen to his voice" (John 10:3). True worship is sometimes silent, not with passive inactivity but with active listening, demonstrating a true desire to know God's heart and plan in every moment.

While often overlooked, gratitude or thanksgiving is also a part of worship. Like most people, we struggle to focus on the good things in life. Somehow, the difficulties manage to steal the lion's share of our attention. We might be living in the wake of numerous blessings, but one challenge or hardship can derail us, even leading us to question God's goodness and power.

That's why thankfulness shows up in the lists of behaviors Paul provides for disciples (Col. 3:12–15). Maintaining an attitude of gratitude must be intentional. There's no question that God's expressions of goodness toward us significantly outnumber our struggles. In fact, He has likely already proven His faithfulness to us in the exact area where we need to trust Him now. That makes our memory a critical tool for a life of worship.

Now some look at a list of behaviors such as these and see the familiar idea of spiritual disciplines. Indeed, these (and a few others) form effective daily patterns of discipleship. But spiritual disciplines divorced from a deepening relationship and a hunger to experience God quickly become formality or a to-do list. Studying the Bible, spending time in prayer, listening to God, or even fasting are not ends in themselves or ways to enhance one's connection to God. They are expressions of a life given to God's purpose. They are the choices of one who has heard that "Whom shall we send?" question from God's heart and responded with hand held high.

This is a life that's lived "out there." The early disciples gathered regularly for worship, but they knew they would only find God's power as they lived each day and embraced His presence. Gatherings with fellow believers weren't the "filling station." A life lived in the marketplace would find its empowering out there, among those God had called them to reach.

That kind of power is needed desperately in every setting and context. Those who live the Spirit-empowered life always have greater impact than those who merely sing the songs. Commitment to mission is the greatest worship of all. Jesus connected love with obedience, and the Bible reminds us that even the Father preferred obedience to sacrifice (1 Sam. 15:22). That's what He meant when He told the Samaritan woman that "his worshipers must worship in the Spirit and in truth" (John 4:24). She wanted to be sure she was attending the right church, but Jesus showed her the deeper issue.

Ultimately, our greatest commandment is to "love the Lord your God with all your heart and with all your soul and with all your mind" and to "love your neighbor as yourself" (Matt. 22:37, 39). Does that sound like something we can achieve on a Sunday morning?

Clearly loving God is going to take all week.

THINK ABOUT IT

1. What likely happens if people who know you see you act one way on Sunday and a different way the rest of the week?
2. How might your commitment to your job be a way to demonstrate the presence of God in your life?

CHAPTER

36

Worship: Obedience, Serving, and Open Doors

For just three small letters, the word *all* sure covers a lot. It's *all* in, *all* inclusive, *all* consuming, and *all* of the above. Nothing gets left out of an *all*. There's no *some* that's excluded. *All* means *all, all* of the time.

So when Jesus says that we must love God with *all* of our heart, soul, mind, and strength, there's really no room for holding any part back. He demands complete, unreserved, and unconditional devotion.

Now, that seems like a tall order, doesn't it? Surely it's a bigger task than most of us think at first. We quickly affirm our love for God and our gratitude for all He has done for us, but we also reserve love for the possessions we've accumulated and the status we've achieved. We do well to love God more than these, but that's still insufficient when compared to the command. That's why Jesus occasionally made some overwhelming statements like "If anyone comes to me and does not hate father and mother, wife and children, brothers and sisters—yes, even their own life—such a person cannot be my disciple" (Luke 14:26). That seems a bit extreme, but given the command, well, it makes sense doesn't it? Who can love God like that?

Those who live Spirit-empowered lives dominate the list of those who try. This is the goal of worship, to give ourselves fully to God and His purposes. Loving God with *all* of one's heart, soul, mind, and strength means prizing nothing but that relationship and yielding all else to His greater wisdom. It can mean a level of sacrifice that is completely inexplicable.

It's a wholehearted love.

So a young woman abandons the education she's fought for, the fiancé who offers security, and the chance for an economic success never before enjoyed in her family to take the message of Christ to people she's never met and barely heard of. A guy sells his business and moves with his wife and children across the globe where they can live and die among people who know nothing of a God of love. No, these aren't stories of missionary heroes from decades past, but sacrifices willingly made in the last few years. And they're not as unusual as you might think.

Loving God wholeheartedly doesn't always mean relocating across the planet. Others step up every day on college campuses, fearlessly risking rejection and marginalization to speak and act on behalf of the One they love. Others take public stands in the business world for what they know is right, serving a God whose ways aren't always interpreted as politically correct or economically advantageous. Yes, there will be lost clients and even damaged reputations, but no sacrifice seems too great for one who loves so deeply.

For the Spirit-empowered, worship comes from the heart. Their songs of praise aren't driven by music tastes or favorite bands. Instead, they connect with passionate words that lyrically express a passion present within. Like the psalmists, they praise from life and worship the God who lives with them every day.

> For the Spirit-empowered, worship comes from the heart.

You see, in the expression of worship, everything comes together for the Spirit-empowered. We love God by loving others; serving them provides a way to serve Him. Loving the unlovely or even the enemy in His name proves a heart of amazing devotion, one that is reshaped daily from selfishness into the heart of Christ.

Obedience marks the heart as well. It's not difficult when commands flow with the grain of preferences or even logical understanding, but ask Abraham what it means to senselessly sacrifice your greatest treasure, the beloved son God promised (Gen. 22:1–11). When God's ways don't mesh comfortably with our ways and we must let go, even of things we're convinced He has given, that's wholehearted love at work.

That same love is demonstrated in sacrificial service—giving of our resources beyond the point of comfort to bring comfort to others. Wholehearted love goes the extra mile, unconcerned about giving more than others might believe they can afford (Matt. 26:9)—whether time, energy, or wealth—knowing that the One loved ultimately has provided everything and can be trusted to do so again.

Finally, that love runs through open doors, careless of inadequacy but knowing that the God who has empowered will equip again. Love equates to trust and active faith, meaning opportunities flow from God's capacity and need not be judged by our own. It's in those moments that demand God and yet require us to step forward where wholehearted love is clearly on display.

This is true worship, a kind of love that is only possible for the Spirit-empowered. Our own determination, no matter how practiced and disciplined, can't measure up. When Jesus said the Holy Spirit would help us worship the Father and the Son, He made clear that without that help, we couldn't fulfill the greatest of commands.

> ## Worship pulls together every element of Spirit-empowered expression.

Worship pulls together every element of Spirit-empowered expression. And it makes sense that this would reveal such a life since relationship with God is at its core. Yes, the power of the Spirit makes possible the greatest of exploits, but it's the intimate connection to God that drives this life. As we have seen, love for God motivates true disciples, bringing the only thing we can offer to an infinite God. And that love, expressed more and more in wholehearted fashion, opens the way for God to pour His power through us.

∞

The Spirit-empowered life is expressed through worship in many forms. It's perhaps most visible in corporate settings where hunger for God extends freedom to Him to pour out His Spirit as He chooses. Though these worship gatherings are often known for unusual moments or unique manifestations, their real character consists in the absolute passion the Spirit-empowered have for deep and life-changing fellowship with God. Yes, at times, this pursuit can be excessive or fleshly, but those with genuine desire to connect with God find Him continually willing to bring such supernatural encounter.

While we celebrate God's presence in worship, the true experience brings His awesome nature into contact with our tragic inadequacy. Like Isaiah, we are taken in by the immensity of His power and majesty but overwhelmed by His holiness. Our failure shines more brightly than we can stand, and we are desperate for what only He can provide—redemption and cleansing that make it possible for us to survive the encounter. Thankfully,

He has extended that mercy toward us, and we not only survive but thrive as He fills us with His power.

Spirit-empowered disciples sense their own unworthiness and willingly confess it, never allowing pride to enter their hearts. Worship can only be expressed through a humility that clearly acknowledges God in His greatness and our absolute need of Him.

And that humility governs more than just Sunday moments of singing praise with others. Every day of the week provides an opportunity to demonstrate a heart of worship. As His people, we know that it is our lives that bring Him the greatest glory. Sundays play a valuable role, providing encouragement and instruction, but the Spirit-empowered take personal responsibility for their growth and pursue that growth every day.

And that growth is demonstrated in many ways. Daily encounters in God's Word and a prayer habit that keeps the relationship fresh and focused show the desire to live in constant communion with God. Learning to hear God's voice proves our genuine passion to find God's path, and gratitude demonstrates our knowledge that He is our Source. Finally, the willingness to move through the doors God opens ahead of us proves that relationship and provides the equipping experiences we need to move forward in His power.

Because of this vibrant approach to life, energy and power are found all week long and growth comes as we pursue our God-given purpose. Sundays aren't our only time for refueling. In fact, the longer we live the Spirit-empowered life, the more "fuel" is found in the marketplace experiences. This is where such a remarkable life is lived, not merely in spiritual expressions amidst church friends. Signs follow those who believe as we run forward with the mission God has given us.

Ultimately, the worship expressed by the Spirit-empowered reveals our wholehearted love for God. Nothing is held back. Jesus told us that God's greatest command is to love Him with all our heart, mind, soul, and strength and to love our neighbor as ourselves. That challenge takes priority in the Spirit-empowered life and generates a growing dedication to God and His purposes, whatever they might require. Nothing else matters.

But such a life cannot be lived without the help of the Holy Spirit. To love God sacrificially and to conquer self-interest goes well beyond human capacity. Paul tells us there is too much of the flesh to overcome on our own (Rom. 7:15). This battle demands a strength greater than our own, and if we yield to God's presence and power, He will help us live the passion of our hearts.

So every moment of our lives can be lived loving, obeying, serving, and pursuing God's mission. This is the nature of worship, the kind of "living sacrifice" that Paul says is our "reasonable" act of service. And that's the true nature of worship—far more than a song list or even an expression of spiritual gifts. Worship is a wholehearted commitment to God and all that He leads us to become. And in that hunger and passion, we find and reveal the relationship that only the Spirit-empowered fully enjoy.

THINK ABOUT IT

1. What does loving God with *all* your heart look like in your life?
2. How might caring for His purposes give you the opportunity to prove that love?
3. How might such an attitude change your life?

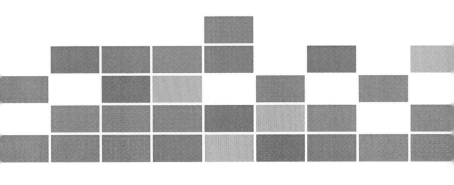

THE HORIZON

CHAPTER 37

Next Steps: Live by Faith

T he righteous will live by faith." Seems simple enough on paper, doesn't it? When Jesus sent His disciples out on their first missional experience, He told them to pack lightly. No suitcases, no extra cash, nothing extra in their pockets (Luke 10:1–10). For those who like to live on the edge, that sounds fun. Those of us who try to plan details in advance might find such an approach a bit unsettling. But clearly, Jesus was setting them up for a journey of complete dependence on God—a journey of faith.

Every disciple needs a working understanding of this spiritual concept because faith matters every single day. It's absolutely essential if we want to please God (Heb. 11:6), and it's the ingredient Jesus was always looking for when creating His miracle recipes.

When Jesus pointed His disciples toward that upper room and insisted that they "stand by" until they had received God's power, no one seems to have told them what to do to receive the promise or what would happen when they did. But they waited, with an expectancy called faith.

Faith is putting our whole weight on what God has said. Jesus said, "Wait," so they waited, fully believing something would occur, even though they didn't know how it might happen. And when the air in that place began moving like a powerful wind and fiery lights enveloped them, they reached up to receive rather than run from the room. Jesus had promised this moment. They had believed what He said and now they embraced it with that same faith.

The Spirit-empowered today encounter this Spirit baptism with similar faith. Believing that Jesus has the same desire to fill us with His power, we wait with expectancy. And though some of the events of the moment may look a bit different (God has many ways of displaying His power), the response is the same—the new tongues, the Spirit's power—every part of His promise is received by faith.

That's not the same as doing something to make it happen. Some, in their eagerness to experience God's promise, think they must design their own windy room, hold their hands a certain way, or begin to craft their own unusual speech to get things started. This isn't faith. It's impatience. The disciples waited for this promise for days. It seems unlikely that God would open a drive-thru window for us. If, in our rush to receive, we buy our own gift, should we be surprised that the power isn't included?

Faith is required. It means believing that God will equip us to do the work we desperately want to engage. Peter told the crowd that this promise was for them and their children (Acts 2:17). God wants each of us to engage His harvest work, so He's not going to limit the distribution of His power to a few. Remember that this kind of faith is believing God will do what He has said He will do.

It's not faith in ourselves. Too many would-be disciples stand behind the wall of their real and perceived limitations. They hear God's heartbeat but look at their

> God wants each of us to engage His harvest work, so He's not going to limit the distribution of His power to a few.

own weak hands and decide they should be disqualified. Sometimes they are intimidated by the power or giftings they see in others. Dreams are the right size, but the hope of living those dreams seems dwarfed by their own inability. So *I can't* becomes *I won't* and before long cements itself in *I never will.*

Let's be honest. If fulfilling God's mission had anything to do with our abilities, God would have needed a new plan long ago. Look at the fellas He chose as His first team. One of the main things we learn from that list of names is the clear idea that this job can fit anyone. I mean no disrespect, Bartholomew, but if you can do it . . .

Faith in ourselves is an unstable proposition, for what we can do fluctuates with our strength, our emotions, and how these connect to daily circumstances. Some days I'm up to the challenge, while other days find me wilting before simple things. Faith in myself leads to fitful starts and stops that don't get me anywhere. But faith in God . . . well, that's the sturdiest of stools to stand on.

Spirit-empowered people also know that faith in faith isn't the answer.

When Jesus spoke of our need for greater faith (Matt. 8:26), it seems He saw faith on a varied scale. But it's probably more of a pass/fail type of measure. When He begged for faith like a mustard seed (17:20), He wasn't speaking solely of size but of durability and hidden strength. Those little seeds prove to be extraordinarily powerful, far beyond what one might expect.

Enough faith means faith to move forward or to step out. We can claim to have faith, but if we don't step out in faith, then our faith is deficient. Ultimately, any measure of the amount of faith we possess would only determine if our faith is sufficient for action. Do we have enough faith to step into the moment God has created for us?

So faith in our faith—the effort to believe harder or more determinedly—misses the point. Many have lost heart when a desired outcome failed to occur, their disappointment magnified by the accusation that they didn't have enough faith or didn't believe hard enough—as if contorting one's eyebrows tightly and clenching fists until blood vessels in the forehead begin to pop will make things happen. That's not faith (and it'll give you a headache).

Faith is believing God will do what He has said, and believing enough to act on it. So, there are really two components—hearing what God has said and responding to His direction. Faith is listening and believing.

We already know that in the Spirit-empowered life, we must learn to hear God's voice, whether through the living pages of His Word or in the seeming whispers of daily moments. Discerning how God may be speaking to our situations through the Bible requires that we understand what He has said and whether or not it applies to our situation. For example, God may speak something to me that He isn't saying to you. He may ask me to attempt what He has not asked you to attempt. In the same way, God spoke things to Samson that He is not speaking to me. To date, I've not been directed to tie foxes together, put torches in their tails, and set them loose in Philistine fields (Judg. 15:4–5). So we discern that some of God's directives, even those we read about in the Bible, aren't meant for all of us. Just because He said it to them doesn't mean He's saying it to me, unless I can see that God's intent stretches to my ears as well.

God can whisper some pretty interesting things. Imagine Simon Peter joining the mourners as they gather to weep over Tabitha's death (Acts 9:36–41). She was a valuable woman to that community, but I wonder if anyone else was thinking what Peter suddenly thought—that God might want to raise her from the dead?

Faith is listening and then believing. Action is required. Peter could have heard God's voice, but there had to be a moment when he stepped forward. As James said, "Faith without deeds is useless" (James 2:20). The whispers of God die out and nothing is achieved for His great purpose.

Faith hears and responds, and the results are often startling. Only by God's voice did Peter know that Ananias was lying about the

Faith hears and responds, and the results are often startling.

selling price of his field (Acts 5:1–4). And only by God's voice did the apostle know what God would do next. But God didn't tell Peter so he could explain the situation after Ananias crumpled to the floor. He gave Peter the ominous words to say that proclaimed judgment on the man, and immediately Ananias died. Then his wife died, as well, when it was her turn to lie. Peter heard and believed enough to speak. Wow! That's a powerful moment.

Whenever we hear God's voice and step out in faith, we find He is there. Even the miraculous can occur when God's plan includes it. But without faith, who will touch the blind eyes or speak words of hope in unlikely circumstances? Yes, God can demonstrate His greatness without us, but He promised His power so we could be a part of His remarkable plan. To miss that is to miss the abundant life He came to give.

Faith isn't knowing what to do; it's knowing the God who will do it. That's why Paul and Barnabas recoiled in horror when the people of one city tried to worship them for the miracles they performed (Acts 14:11–18). They knew the voice of God and the powerless truth about their lives without Him. They knew that God alone could do what had been done. They had only listened and obeyed, good acts in themselves but hardly a reason to be worshipped.

A life of faith isn't always one of clear and easy steps. Some think that those who live Spirit-empowered lives constantly overflow with steady confidence and nonstop assurance. But faith has many uncertain steps. We learn to hear God's voice more clearly as our relationship with Him grows, but even distant moments when that relationship has reached a high level of maturity will still require faith. And every moment will insist that we trust a power and voice not our own.

THINK ABOUT IT

1. How has faith stirred you to step out and make a difference with your life?
2. What tends to get in your way most often when you try to live by faith?
3. To what degree have you tried to live as a disciple in your own strength?

CHAPTER 38

Next Steps:
Think Mission

I t's all about mission! For many, the terms *mission* or *missional* have lost their meaning. Over the past decade or so, these words have joined the ranks of the over-used. Everyone has a mission, whether it's a dentist's office, a hair salon, or the taco shop down the street. Apparently, you can't be cool unless you've discovered your mission and displayed it in an attractive wall hanging.

A clear sense of mission is a good thing, even if one isn't aiming for life-changing results. But some clock out of their mission every afternoon to head home and live free of such focus. Not the Spirit-empowered. Ours is an eternal assignment from which we never retire, a joyous pursuit that grows more remarkable each day. It's a vital mission—no poster needed.

When we speak of the mission of the Spirit-empowered, we know our directive is crafted by an all-wise and perfect God. He provides the direction, the presence, and the power to get the job done. All that's missing is our willing response. Like eighty-five-year-old Caleb in the Old Testament, divine strength is available to help us conquer amazing challenges. God is just waiting for us to say, "Give me this hill country" (Josh. 14:10–12).

That's how the Spirit-empowered live. If only that mentality were a bit more widespread among modern worshippers. You see, when it comes to engaging mission, people respond at three levels. Most of us travel through each of these, growing deeper in our commitment as we grow in our relationship with God. Sadly, some folks don't progress as they could, or even as many of us think they should. But each level comes with its own stage of understanding, and its own level of intent.

The first of these is what we might call a *consumer* level of missional engagement. Actually, at this level there isn't much engagement at all. As the title implies, this is a place where people enjoy the blessings of God's presence in their neighborhood, but they remain . . . well, the nice word might be *self-focused.*

These folks likely attend church services—even regularly. They greet each moment with a desire to receive whatever the local church might deliver that week. So times of worship are embraced, especially when they generate good feelings and a sense of connection to God.

"Great message, Pastor. You gave me a lot to think about. Thanks for coming to my kid's ballgame. He's got another on Friday if you've got the time. Oh, and my aunt is near death, and we're going to need someone to do the funeral. It's only about an hour from here and, well, you're the only pastor we know." This, or something similar, is the usual conversational content with the consumer.

> Much of what we long for in the Spirit-empowered life is the opportunity and ability to see more lives impacted in even more remarkable ways as we bring God's resources to those in need.

Now don't misunderstand. There's absolutely nothing wrong with the local church ministering to these and many other needs. It's what we do, isn't it? Caring for needs is a huge part of loving people, and we're glad when folks connect those dots. Much of what we long for in the Spirit-empowered life is the opportunity and ability to see more lives impacted in even more remarkable ways as we bring God's resources to those in need. No, there's absolutely nothing wrong with bringing our needs to Him. It's part of the plan!

It's just that some people never progress beyond the *consumer* mentality.

Yes, God is willing to meet our needs no matter how long we've been connected to Him, but there should come a time when we begin to understand that this journey isn't just about us. It's about Him and the life mission He has for us.

Jesus showed some weariness with crowds that were unwilling to move past consumer ideas and into real faith. He questioned those who came back the day after He miraculously fed them those fish and loaves. He complained that people were "ever seeing but never perceiving" (Matt. 13:14). Clearly by believing, He meant more than just agreeing that He was God. Even the demons know that for sure (James 2:19). To Jesus, believing means choosing to follow Him, to want to know what He wants and then to give our full effort to that. Some consumers never seem to get there.

I call the second level of engagement a *ministry* response. These people are the willing helpers in the kingdom of God. At some point, they lay aside their consumer thinking and offer to help when they hear about a need. So someone mentions a need for help with the children on Sunday or an opening on the usher team. The teenagers need a teacher (the last one disappeared). Could someone bring donuts? There are many possible ministries to get involved in at church, and most could sure use one more worker, so churches try to help each person discover their unique abilities in hopes that they'll get the hint to start using them.

Ministry people take the hint and begin to do their part. They help, and every pastor is grateful they do. Without them, we couldn't manage the ministry effort.

But there's still a bit of the consumer at work here. Now when the pastor talks to them, the conversation isn't just about "How are you doing?" but he wants to know "How is it going? How did the children's class go this morning? Isn't ushering fun? Can you see how important the work among our teenagers really is? Which donut shop is your favorite?" The questions no longer center on the individual's personal needs but focus more on how the effort to help is unfolding. Why? Because their pastor wants them to have a good ministry experience and keep growing in their personal journey with God. And . . . he doesn't want them to quit. If they do, he'll have to find someone else to bring donuts.

Things don't get missional until the third stage. In fact, I call this the *missional* level. Here people have engaged the mission. They know why they do what they do and believe strongly in that purpose. In fact, at this level, people live the mission even without a specific assignment. They find a way to make a difference and care deeply about the purpose of everything they do. Missional people are a pastor's best friends because they're self-motivated. They hear their leader's heart and meaningfully respond. These folks still have needs, but they don't lose focus on the bigger picture. They trust God to care for their struggles as they give themselves more fully to the struggles of others. Missional people "get it."

Now you can probably see the possible progression. Most people come to Jesus with some sort of need and connect with Him in order to receive and consume His goodness. From there, they begin to get involved, helping where needed and slowly becoming less consumed with their own benefit. And somewhere in their volunteer effort their heart begins to break for the mission. They've seen God's power alter the lives around them, and they want to be a part of that all the time.

Unfortunately, the consumers all too often outnumber the missional. Among most faith communities, about two-thirds of the people are currently at the *consumer* level while 25–30 percent have engaged the *ministry* phase. Do the math and you'll see that the head count of the *missional* is the smallest group. And the ratios seldom change, even when more people adopt the mission. You see, the more *missional* folks there are in a church, the more *consumer* folks they are connected with and the more *ministry* efforts are needed. More *missional* disciples means more of the others as well.

Now you may wonder why we would discuss these remedial levels near the end of a book like this. After all, shouldn't the Spirit-empowered have settled into the missional family long ago? How can such a question be part of the "next steps" when that life has been fully engaged? The answer is in the importance of maintaining that intent. Somehow it's possible to be fully committed to the mission of Christ at one point, but then lose that focus and drift back toward the consumer end of the scale. That might seem unlikely (and it's certainly not desired), but some healthy disciples succumb to an inward focus over time and lose track of the outward passion that once drove them. Some local churches even contend with this spiritual regression among their leaders. And when that happens, things won't be healthy for long.

> The Spirit-empowered find renewal and growth by pursuing the mission of God.

The Spirit-empowered find renewal and growth by pursuing the mission of God. As we encounter opportunities to demonstrate His love and strength, we find more strength ourselves. To drift to the sidelines means more than lost momentum. Things can deteriorate more quickly than we might imagine, so a determined focus into the future is absolutely critical.

Jesus said that anyone who "puts a hand to the plow and looks back" is not worthy of His kingdom (Luke 9:62). That's a frightening possibility that must be guarded against at all costs. The Spirit-empowered must understand our potential for such stumbling so we can guard against it and encourage one another to maintain clear focus.

It's our connection to other missional people that can provide that needed encouragement. Pastors need missional people, and missional people need one another. When Jesus prepared to launch His Commission, He told His group to "Love one another" (John 13:34–35). In fact, He moved that command to the top of their list.

Why? Because He knew the resistance they would face and He knew the temptation to give up would pay regular visits. It seems God's favorite number is two, because He made us interdependent on one another. In fact, Jesus even said that when "two or three gather in my name, there am I with them" (Matt. 18:20). Now there's a reason to stick together!

Against the backdrop of a consumer world, a missional life shines brightly. The Spirit-empowered live with the greatest purpose, one that brings hope to our own lives as powerfully as it glows for the broken. Self-centered living leads to aloneness, but we who fully engage God's mission find ourselves among the most remarkable family. We live lives of power, purpose, and remarkable Presence. We are finding an abundant life more and more each day.

THINK ABOUT IT

1. How have you seen a bit of inward focus creep into your own life?
2. Do you see yourself at the consumer, ministry, or missional stage?
3. What steps can you take to move to the next level or more fully solidify your place at the highest stage?

CHAPTER
39

Next Steps: Engage the Moments

In my part of the world, we call it *rubbernecking*. This odd word describes people who gawk at and ogle the events that surround them . . . but they never stop to get involved. A surprisingly high number of traffic jams are caused by this seemingly innocuous behavior. People slow down to see but never stop to offer help.

Rubbernecking has become a most common and assumed behavior in our times. We see the accident, the crisis, the titillating story unfolding around us, but we don't get close enough to risk expectation. "*Don't get involved*" is the easy mantra, because involvement gets complicated, even risky at times.

Jesus knew something about rubbernecking. In fact, He told a powerful story about a couple of guys who had this behavior down to a science. In His parable about a man who was overtaken by the perils of the road to Jericho (a road that's still not suitable for a Sunday drive), Jesus introduced us to a priest and a Levite—two guys who had been tasked with missional lives by God Himself (Luke 10:30–35). Unfortunately for the guy who "was attacked by robbers," these men saw their mission as somewhere other than their shared moment. They looked . . . they clearly saw . . . and they crossed to the other side of the road. I've seen that road and it's not a four-lane highway. It's a footpath. The other side was only a step or two away.

Jesus' point, of course, is the guy who did stop, and He made Him a Samaritan to add to His point. But regardless of the man's distasteful identity (to those listening from the front row), the story brought an easy and clear answer to the question that had prompted it: *Who is my neighbor?*

Jesus' answer went beyond the expected. Neighbors—the recipients of our commanded love—extend beyond the backyard fence and block party participants. Clearly they even exceed the limited list of people we know and like. The story of the Good Samaritan shows us that neighbors are the people who surround us in thousands of moments every single day. They could be anybody because they are everybody. People of Jesus' kingdom don't just look—they get involved. I'm not sure if there's an Aramaic or Hebrew word for rubbernecking, but Jesus' story says stop it.

We who live Spirit-empowered lives understand that the life we hunger for comes to us in moments. God shapes circumstances around us that open doors to the love and power He has placed within us. Like Peter and John in Acts 3, lame men appear on the temple steps before us waiting for the power we've been given—waiting for us to engage them.

> God shapes circumstances around us that open doors to the love and power He has placed within us.

There will be moments. Jesus made that clear.

He told His disciples there would be moments when they would be "arrested and brought to trial" (Mark 13:11)—clearly moments they would not choose for themselves—but that the Holy Spirit would provide the words they would need to address their accusers. (There's another proof of the "freely receive, freely give" experience, isn't it?) The point is that whether a supernatural healing event, a chance to bind up the broken, or even a handcuff-laden encounter with the authorities, there will be moments for the Spirit-empowered life to shine through.

You need to be ready to engage such moments.

There's the challenge. If you want to live a Spirit-empowered life, you have to move toward those moments, and when you do, the power God has placed within you is on the remarkable verge of display. Peter and John saw the lame man, and something inside them said, "Look at us!" Peter bravely repeated what he heard, and the rest is quite an amazing history.

I find it interesting that the first responses to the Spirit's power in the book of Acts were expressions of boldness. In Acts 2, Peter boldly stepped forward to explain the remarkable events occurring in that upper room, and healing the lame man took some bold moves as well. And that miracle landed Peter and John in front of the religious ruling body in Acts 4, where they asserted that their suspicious audience was guilty in the death of the One by whose power they had just healed. Boy, when Jesus promised the

Holy Spirit would give them words to say . . . wow, that was bold!

Later in that same chapter, the other believers marveled at Peter and John's experience before the Sanhedrin and realized they needed boldness, too. So they prayed. They didn't engage a three-week study on boldness or buy a book from the boldest of the bold. They prayed, and the Holy Spirit shook the place as He filled their hearts with . . . boldness (Acts 4:23–31).

If you want to live a Spirit-empowered life, you must first experience the Spirit's power, but then you must engage the moments life brings you every day. You cannot know the potential in each conversation. You cannot imagine the possibilities as you step into someone else's brokenness. But you cannot live a life of power from the sidelines. Words like *connect, grow, serve,* and *go* aren't the stuff of spectators.

So what's behind that boldness? For the Spirit-empowered, there's an expectation that God will step into those moments with us.

In 1 Corinthians 12, Paul mentions a number of ways that God does that, a list that we call spiritual gifts. God's plan to pour in so we can pour out is clearly seen as He invests what we need in every moment we face. He has wisdom, knowledge, and discernment at the ready. Supernatural faith, healings, and other miracles are in His treasure box, too. He'll speak to us by speaking through us in prophetic power, and we find an amazing strength when we speak back to Him in the Spirit-driven language He has placed within our hearts.

> The Spirit-empowered step into each day, expecting to encounter a purpose greater than ourselves authored by the only One who could make such things happen.

Our boldness isn't generated by human determination. We can expect that God has arrived in our moments even before we're on the scene, and that He will equip us for whatever He seeks to achieve. Freely receive, freely give works really well when the One with the power has the plan.

So Spirit-empowered people actively expect and seek these gifts of the Spirit. We look to God for wisdom and insight into every circumstance. We put our full weight on God's ability and desire to show Himself in miracles that bear His signature. We anticipate that God will give us words to proclaim

His love and purpose, and like Paul, we communicate intimately with God in the language we know and the one only He knows (1 Cor. 14:15, 18).

The Spirit-empowered step into each day, expecting to encounter a purpose greater than ourselves authored by the only One who could make such things happen. That's why He gets all the attention. Sure, there have been a few that sink into drawing attention to themselves. Paul dealt with that in his day (Phil. 1:15), and it's reasonable to expect such people will turn up in every generation. But when we know where such a powerful life truly originates, it's hard to imagine any reason for things to go to our heads.

Frankly, if you've made it all the way to this chapter, I can't imagine that you're still a bystander in the quest for the life we've been describing. There's a life of power and impact for you to receive, but you have to believe in God's plan if you're going to receive it.

Not sure where to start? Remember that the Spirit-empowered life always starts with experience—the place where you receive what God wants you to give. Start each day seeking the boldness and power of God's Spirit that will guide your eyes and ears to the moments you'll encounter that day.

Then engage.

Look for an opportunity to *meet* someone you've never met. Each day your life is filled with nameless people—the girl at the dry cleaners, the guy who's making your burrito, the bank teller, and the neighbor kid who left his bike blocking your driveway. *Meet* one of those people every day. Engage their stories, understand their struggles, and try to see life through their eyes. Too many Christians try to share the gospel like a vacuum cleaner salesman tries to prove his product's superior suction power. Throw away the script and engage someone else's world. It's a lot easier to know what to say if you listen first.

Of course, you can engage those you already know, too. The point is that you want to know, you want to hear, and you want to care. And like an ancient Samaritan Jesus once introduced, you want to bind up the wounds that everyone else just gawks at as they drive by. Stop ignoring your neighbors and engage them. *Meet* them like you never have before. Remember that Jesus came from heaven to earth for us, but some people won't find Him until you cross the street for them.

Look for an opportunity to *pray* with others when you hear their needs. The Spirit-empowered know where our help comes from, and we are quick to confess that Source so others can learn to seek Him, too. The old adage hasn't grown rusty with age—*prayer changes things*. Why can't you engage that coworker by praying over his crumbling marriage? Why can't you pray with a classmate just before you both face a critical exam? What might happen if you asked God to step into your neighbor's financial mess? Peter and John didn't sit down on the temple steps to discuss their views on lameness or demonstrate their own proven skill in walking. They pointed the man to the extraordinary name of Jesus! That's what started the dance party.

Look for an opportunity to *help* someone every day. That's how Jesus lived. He came to serve, and the opportunities came His way in droves. Surprise people with kindness. Go the extra mile. Sacrifice some time and energy for someone else's to-do list. You'll rarely hear, "Mind your own business" when you're truly there to help.

Meet, pray, help. It's a simple strategy to begin engaging the moments God has been crafting around you. I like to call it MPH, because it reminds me of the familiar use of those three letters on my car's dashboard—*miles per hour.* As you *meet, pray,* and *help* people every day, you'll find your Spirit-empowered life will begin picking up speed.

Some will resist such bold action, fearing they don't have what someone else's moment will require. Others will insist that such movement doesn't fit their natural personality. But that's the beauty of the Spirit-empowered life. You don't have to master the moments before you step up. God gives you what He wants you to give others. You'll find exactly what's needed to feed someone else by looking in your own lunch box. In fact, sometimes you won't even know what He's given you until you open your mouth to speak.

Engage the moments of every day and you'll see how God multiplies what you have to feed the lives of the hundreds and thousands you're willing to engage. You will receive power . . . and you will be . . .

This is the life you want.

THINK ABOUT IT

1. What might most easily get in the way of you engaging opportunities for daily impact?
2. Can you describe a moment you may have missed recently? What kept you from embracing that opportunity?
3. Who have you met in the last week? Who have you met in the last month?

C H A P T E R

40

Next Steps: Write New Stories

There are more stories to write . . . *but first they must be lived*. Pages ago, we began this book with stories of common men doing uncommon things. Gideon's unlikely victory, Samson's great feats of strength, and David's surprising bravery wrote the stories of their lives, and each was defined by a simple phrase—*the Spirit of the Lord was upon them*.

Theirs and the stories of dozens of others bring the wisdom of the Bible to livable reality, for each tale of greatness shows what can happen when God connects with the likes of us.

But while stories such as these provide a template of possibilities, we didn't come to our subject in search of stories already lived. Instead, we're hungry for the ones yet ahead, those that are even now lining up on the path before us. We're hungry for Spirit-empowered lives, and we're confident God is still crafting those.

We want more!

But that desire isn't born of pride or a fascination with the sensational. This hunger emerges from want and need. We long for the maximum life God can create in us for His purpose, and we know that our times are desperate for someone to find that life. This day is as ripe for a display of God's power as any.

You'd think that with centuries of scientific discovery under our belts and a technological prowess that grows more impressive with every new product release we might have figured out how to live. Sure, we can do more in our twenty-four globe spins than our ancestors, but there's no connection between achievement and quality living. We can do, but we still can't seem to be.

Given our planet's amazing resources and the transportation genius that traverses the known world, you'd think hunger would be a problem of the past. Yet millions are still starving, some even within the borders of the wealthiest of nations. Organizations pop up everywhere to build water wells in the Third World—a really good idea. It's just that given how we have always needed water like we need air, you'd think we would have started a bit sooner.

Slavery seems as prevalent as ever. No, it's not a right defended by leading nations anymore, but it may have grown worse—if that could be possible. Today, slavery involves children sold for sex, destroying their young lives through despicable trafficking. And it's not just those places needing clean water that violate humanity in such ways. Indeed, the well-building nations fully share in the guilt on this front.

It's now been a century since the "war to end all wars" was fought. It didn't. In fact, barbarous activity may be at an all-time high, or at least we now have the media reach to bring every gory detail to our laptops. Hatred and violence still rule national and international news, and our advanced weaponry seems within easy reach of the worst perpetrators. It's high time someone really big screamed, "Stop it!" at all of us.

It would take another book to identify all the sources of brokenness and devastation that merge into a single news cycle. But that's not our point. Suffice it to say, we're expanding and manufacturing on a level unknown to human history, but we're not any better at living, and the blackness of sin's spread is as dark as ever.

That's why we need more stories.

Jesus came as a light to this dark place. His was a message of hope and restoration, an Eden-like possibility for those who wanted to discover and journey with God. He brought a kingdom of love and the security only an eternal and infinite God could offer. And that message still travels the globe with those who have taken Him at His word.

They are the Spirit-empowered—men, women, and even the young— who live on a different plane, and their stories bring change where it couldn't be found anywhere else. These have discovered a path that brings the vibrant back to life. Theirs is an adventure greater than the movie scripts that stretch imaginations.

And more such people are wanted and needed.

A lot of them are already out there, making a difference with stories that fly under the radar of the broadcast entities. But those finding hope in their hands know the impact they're making.

- Three little boys who lost their dad grew up knowing the daily sting of hunger. Together they've spent their adult years piloting one of the world's fastest growing relief organizations and now feed tens of thousands every day. Their semis of supplies are among the first to arrive on site in times of natural disaster, bringing hope in ways few little boys ever imagine.

- A man and his wife lay aside their own comfort to care for homeless folks in the inner city. The socks they give to those in need provide a warmth for the feet that has a way of surging all the way to the heart. Who knew socks could do that?

- A woman who knows the deep pain and regret that her "right to choose" allowed now brings hope and help to others on that same path. Who could dream of healing such deep-set hurts?

- A high school boy celebrates his miracle healing from cancer by telling his whole football team about the One who healed him. His life affects a city, and many of his teammates connect with a God who gives strength that can't be generated in a weight room. Suffering can bring amazing results.

- A congregation breaks out of its comfortable suburban campus and begins meeting for dinner in communities that other churches have abandoned. These weekly meals embrace people who would never have made it to church. Who ever thought Jesus would be ladling lasagna and breaking bread with the likes of them?

There are thousands more, and their stories likely dominate the games of "show and tell" that angels play at their parties. These are the lives heaven celebrates as the greatness of God shows up on street corners throughout the whole earth.

> These are the lives heaven celebrates as the greatness of God shows up on street corners throughout the whole earth.

I could tell more or even offer the expanded details of the stories I've mentioned. That would be a great way to end a book such as this. After all, I started with some ancient stories so it would be fun to read some modern ones. And their details would prove that such a powerful life is still within reach of those who hunger after God today. Yes, that would be a great way to spend this final chapter.

But frankly, there's a better way.

In fact, there's only one way a book about the Spirit-empowered life should conclude, and that's with the story you are about to write. How will God use you? What will you find Him directing and equipping you to do with your brief decades that remain before eternity takes over? How will you demonstrate the love and power of God in your Jerusalem, Judea, Samaria, or ends-of-the-earth places?

Instead of spending more time rejoicing over what others are doing, I've decided that this will be my book's shortest chapter. I want to leave room for you to write your story. (For help to begin writing your story, please see the page of resources at the end of this book.)

But, you'll have to live it first . . . so start doing that now. Take your want and need to God and let Him magnify your relationship together. He'll give you His power and the moments in His presence that you'll need so you can start giving what you have received.

It's time for you to engage the Spirit-empowered life!

Endnotes

1. Eugene Peterson, *Run with Horses: The Quest for Life at Its Best*
   Downers Grove, IL: InterVarsity Press, 1983), 14.

2. From a sermon given by Dr. Lamar Vest, former General Overseer for
   the Church of God, Cleveland, Tennessee.

About the Author

Mike Clarensau is a freelance writer living in the Dallas area where he also serves as Dean of the College of Bible and Church Ministries for Southwestern Assemblies of God University. He has authored more than a dozen books including, *From Belonging to Becoming*, *Journey to Integrity*, *The Sanctity of Life*, and coauthored *Give Them What They Want*, and *We Build People*. He is a frequent speaker for camps, conferences, and churches across the nation.

Mike and his wife, Kerry, previously spent a decade serving as lead pastors of Maranatha Worship Center in Wichita, Kansas, where they helped guide the revitalization of the church from an aging congregation of around 180 to a vibrant worship community of 750, filled with young adults and more than 55 different nations of birth.

Mike has also filled various national and district roles for the Assemblies of God, serving as director of church health, editor in chief, head of the National Sunday School department, and Youth and Christian Education Director for the denomination's Kansas district.

Mike and Kerry's two sons are both married and they currently have two beautiful granddaughters.

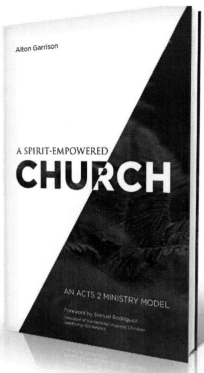

A SPIRIT-EMPOWERED LIFE SMALL GROUPS:

CONNECT, GROW, SERVE, GO, WORSHIP

We are inspired by stories of incredible salvations and mind-blowing ministry of the Holy Spirit, but how do we move from being inspired to actually experiencing these things in our own lives? How do we invite the Holy Spirit to take our spiritual lives to this next level of power and effectiveness?

A Spirit-Empowered Life small group kits lead participants to a deeper understanding of how Holy Spirit-empowerment makes an extraordinary difference in our lives. The DVD offers engaging teaching segments and testimonies featuring personal stories. The coordinating Study Guide provides easy-to follow Bible studies and daily devotions. There are four sessions per kit.

These small group resources are available in English for adults and youth and in Spanish for adults.

Find out more and order a copy today at
MYHEALTHYCHURCH.COM/SPIRITEMPOWERED